# Gone But Not Forgotten

## Coping With Bereavement After Dementia

By Tracy Gough

Gone But Not Forgotten

*Coping With Bereavement After Dementia*

First published in 2020



ISBN-13: 978-1-9999838-2-6

*This book is dedicated to Dawn and Debbie who lost their beloved mum Shirley to dementia.*

# 'Tis Only We Who Grieve

*They do not leave*
*They are not gone.*
*They look upon us still*
*They walk among the valleys now.*
*They stride upon the hill*
*Their smile is in the summer sky.*
*Their grace is in the breeze*
*Their memories whisper in the grass,*
*Their calm is in the trees.*
*Their light is in the winter snow*
*Their tears are in the rain.*
*Their merriment runs in the brook*
*Their laughter in the lane.*
*Their gentleness is in the flowers*
*They sigh in Autumn leaves.*
*They do not leave, they are not gone*
*'Tis only we who grieve.*

~ Author Unknown

# CONTENTS

# INTRODUCTION

I am a Registered Nurse, Life Coach and Author with over 30 years' experience of working in the care sector. During this time, I have mainly worked with people who have dementia. I can personally relate to the impact that dementia has on all concerned as I have been affected by this illness in my own family too.

I still work as a nurse as well as running my own business called 'Make Way for Tomorrow'. The nature of my business is to provide one to one and group support for those who have loved ones with dementia and those going through a bereavement following the death of a loved one to dementia.

My first book 'My Dementia Journey....One step at a time' was released in May 2018 and contains information, tips and advice on dementia. It also has space for family and carers to write their reflective thoughts regarding their own dementia journey and the impact it is having on them and their loved one.

My second book 'Gone But Not Forgotten' has been written to provide support and guidance for those who are going through a bereavement of a loved one, following a dementia illness. This can have a marked effect on all those involved, triggering a variety of emotions and is frequently described as feeling like a 'double bereavement'.

You may have started an initial bereavement process while your loved one was still living because as dementia progresses the person affected often becomes unrecognisable and loses the character that you once knew. A second bereavement inevitably occurs when the end of their life is reached and your loved one unfortunately passes away. It is not unusual and is completely normal for you to go through a mixture of emotions during both bereavements. Losing the one you love 'twice' is extremely difficult and often traumatic.

How we grieve and come to terms with our loss is a unique process. No one can put a time scale on when you will start to feel better, as you may feel like you have been on a continual emotional rollercoaster since your loved one was diagnosed. It is essential that you give yourself time, as some days will appear easier to get through than others. Even though their illness has now ended, it is not unusual to be left reflecting on past events or dwelling on the more difficult times that you endured.

I regularly work with families who are battling to come to terms with the impact that dementia has had on them and their loved one. It is not always easy to put the pieces of your life back together due to the nature of the illness and subsequent bereavement that follows. Your journey may still feel like an uphill struggle as there is often limited support for caregivers going through the loss of a loved one to dementia. It was with this in mind that I decided to write 'Gone But Not Forgotten'.

Use this book as your companion and guide, as you continue to work through your loss. A key message I wanted to convey in 'Gone But Not Forgotten', was that the thoughts and feelings you are now experiencing are completely normal. Be reassured that we will all experience some form of bereavement in our lives. How we can cope and move on will affect us differently.

'Gone But Not Forgotten' like 'My Dementia Journey... One step at a time' can also be used as a reflective diary. It can be your 'place of safety' to write your feelings down openly, away from any judgement or criticism. Reflective thought can help you gain clarity, as well as providing you with an aide to letting go of any frustrations and anger that you may still be holding on to.

I've endeavoured when writing this book to reach as wide an audience as possible, by discussing a variety of areas. Some of these areas may not appear relevant or even sit comfortably with you; this is of course fine. Concentrate on those ones that move you forward and ease your grief. Throughout each section is a selection of meaningful quotes and thought-provoking verses. Revisit and remember the ones that comfort you during this stressful time of your life.

'Gone But Not Forgotten' is split into five sections. The first section discusses the events leading up to your loved one's death and the impact it has had on you. The next two sections explore the different stages of grief and some of the emotions experienced during a bereavement, including past events that may have had a significant effect on you, both during and after your dementia journey. The last two sections are aimed to help you find comfort in your time of grief, with a focus of moving your life forward.

The 'Make Way For Tomorrow' logo dragonfly has once again been used on the front cover. It is there to represent you and your transformation as you bravely travel through your bereavement. The colourful dragonfly and rainbow symbolise peace and hope, to take with you on your forward journey, into your future.

*'We bereaved are not alone. We belong to the largest company in the world – the company of those who have known suffering.'*

~ Helen Keller

# Section 1

## When the Journey has Ended…What Now?

*Those we love don't go away,*

*They walk beside us every day.*

*Unseen, unheard, but always near,*

*Still loved, still missed and very dear.*

~ Author Unknown

# The Long-Term Impact of an Illness like Dementia

When a loved one is diagnosed with dementia, it has a huge impact on the person as well as the lives of all those involved. Watching someone go through this disease can be heart-breaking as often you are faced with watching them lose their memory, personality and the ability to look after themselves. Towards the end of a dementia illness, the person themselves are often frail and have very little recognition of who they are and the life they have lived. You may have spent time experiencing a rollercoaster of emotions, as you stepped into a journey of the unknown. You were possibly faced with coming to terms with your own feelings as well as the reaction to the illness experienced by other members of your family and close friends. What to expect in the future was probably uncertain as well as difficult to comprehend.

If you are reading this book because you have unfortunately lost a loved one to dementia, a lot of what is written above will resonate with you. The fact that you have lived through this dementia journey to the end, must now feel like you have lost your loved one twice and consequently going through the experience of a 'double' bereavement. Living through the process of two bereavements can be challenging, heart-breaking and stressful for all concerned.

Your initial grieving may have occurred while your loved one was still living, because of the effects that the illness had on them. You may have seen many physical changes during this time, and this may have been especially so towards the end of their life. For example, they may have declined food or had difficulty swallowing, causing severe weight loss. Having dementia may have caused your loved one to have developed a completely different personality to the one you used to know. For example, they may have become quick-tempered and frustrated a lot during their dementia illness, which they would have never done previously. Socially they may have become withdrawn and depressed when at one time they were perhaps the 'life and soul of the party' always enjoying the company of others.

The relationship you had with your loved one may have taken on a completely different role as their illness advanced. For instance, they may have become as dependent on you for all their basic needs like you would expect a young child to be.

These are just a few examples of how dementia can have a life-changing impact on all those involved. What was your own personal experience of your loved one's illness?

# Write any thoughts you may have....

# What was the hardest part of the illness for you?

Dementia often leaves an imprint on the lives of all those affected by the illness.

## What effect did your loved one's illness have on the rest of your family and friends?

# Events Leading Up to Your Loved One's Death

Your loved one during the last stages of their dementia may have appeared like a 'shell' of their former self, as everyday functions like eating and drinking, communication and recognition of who people are, often start to diminish.

This end phase can be very cruel and often difficult to endure. During this time, you may have experienced a fluctuation in your own feelings. Perhaps you had moments when you were 'willing' your loved one to die peacefully, to free them and you from their suffering. On other occasions you may have been urging them not to go, knowing that the time you now had left with them was coming to an end.

What was your own experience of events leading up to your loved one's death?

## Write any thoughts you may have below...

______________________________________________

______________________________________________

Maybe your loved one didn't get to the end stages of their dementia but instead passed away more suddenly from perhaps a chronic or unexpected illness.

This happened in the case of my step grandmother. She had dementia but was taken more suddenly than we expected from a chest infection that led to pneumonia. It was a shock to lose her so quickly, even though she'd had dementia for several years and was being looked after in a care home.

Once we had come to terms with her sudden death, it was a relief in hindsight to know that she had not gone on to suffer with the end stages of the illness. Thankfully her slipping away was peaceful with me holding her hand and under the circumstances I could not have wished for anything else.

## Was this similar to your own experience? If so, how do you feel about this now?

*'For death is no more than a turning of us over from time to time to eternity.'*

~ William Penn

# At The Time Of Death

Where was your loved one at the time of their death? Were they being cared for in their own home or possibly a family member's house? Alternatively, they may have been in a care setting like a hospital, hospice or care home.

Was this their expected place to pass away? What were your thoughts about where they were, and the end of life care they received? Was it well managed by the professionals involved?

If you unfortunately felt that things didn't go well, these thoughts can stay with you and subsequently can have a significant impact on your bereavement. It is not uncommon to hear of cases where loved ones have had poor symptom control or a lack of basic care needs.

Alternatively, as a grieving relative, you may have thought that you were not supported by the care organisation or the professionals looking after your loved one. Perhaps you felt that you could not express your concerns to them or that they provided little comfort to you when you needed it most.

Hopefully, you never went on to experience any of the above and that your loved one passed away peacefully with excellent care being given to them, with a lot of support being offered to you too, by dedicated professionals that were a great source of comfort at the end.

## Write any thoughts you may have, on what has been discussed above...

What went as well as could be expected, at the time of your loved one's death?

## What didn't go as well as you expected, at the time of your loved one's death?

___________________________________________

___________________________________________

___________________________________________

___________________________________________

___________________________________________

___________________________________________

___________________________________________

___________________________________________

___________________________________________

___________________________________________

___________________________________________

Were you with your loved one when they passed away? If not was this through your own choice or was the end of their life unexpected?

Throughout my nursing career, I have experienced relatives keeping a vigil at their loved one's bed only to go out for some fresh air and find that within minutes their loved one had passed away without them there. Coming to terms with this can be challenging and especially difficult to comprehend when you have perhaps stayed with them for the last few days and hours of their life.

There are also occasions when people pass away more quickly than anticipated. I have also found myself contacting families to ask them to come in due to a deterioration in their loved one, only for them to take their last breaths, minutes before their family arrive. If this has happened to you, you may have been left feeling guilty or struggling to accept that you didn't get there in time. I urge you not to dwell on this thought because none of us can predict when someone's final moments will be.

Perhaps your loved one clung on to their life for longer than you would have liked them to, especially if they had little in the way of food or drink in their final days. This situation can be stressful and emotionally draining, for all concerned. It may have been difficult at the time to accept that your loved one would only pass over when it was the right time for them.

Watching a loved one at the end of their life can be very frightening, as we never quite know what to expect. You may have felt that the whole experience was quite traumatic or perhaps it was very peaceful.

Death and its final moments are not for everyone and some people choose not to be there at the end. If this applies to you, try not to feel inadequate or guilty about making this choice, even if those around you did not respect or understand your decision to do this.

Whatever your own experience was, it is now essential to search for some form of comfort following your loved one's death. This may be an acknowledgement that they are no longer suffering and that their final breath was a release for them to go to a place of peace or a belief that they are now reunited with other family members who have previously passed away.

## Write any thoughts you may have in the space below...

The death of your loved one may have left you with a mixture of regret and remorse. Perhaps there were things left unsaid, due to not being with them at the end or because you thought your loved one with dementia would not understand.

Whatever your own personal circumstances are, it is important to acknowledge how you are now feeling in order to move on with your own life. To assist you to do this, it may help you to write a letter to your loved one, as though they are still with you. Time spent opening up, can enable you to pour your heart out and be up front with your feelings, as well as telling them everything you would have liked them to have known if they were still living.

Alternatively, if it feels more comfortable, try talking to your loved one as though they are sitting next to you. Find a quiet time or tranquil area, perhaps their favourite place or at their graveside. Take this opportunity to really open-up and express your feelings. If it feels appropriate speak out loud, if not then quietly express any thoughts through your own inner voice.

## You may want to use the space below, to write about the type of things you would have liked your loved one to have known...

---

---

*'Death leaves a heartache no one can heal,*

*Love leaves a memory no one can steal.'*

~ (from a headstone in Ireland)

# Were You Ready to Let Go?

Were you ready at the time of your loved one's death to let them go? It is not unusual to fluctuate between wanting your loved one to live forever but at the same time urging them to be released from an often-cruel illness like dementia.

You may have experienced physical and mental exhaustion towards the end of their life, as you battle with saying goodbye. Especially if they were very poorly for several days and even weeks leading up to their death. During this time, we often don't take care of ourselves, as we are least focused on our own wellbeing, with escalating anxiety, stress and loss of appetite. As a consequence, we are often left feeling exhausted and fatigued. It is not unusual to experience a minor illness like a stomach bug or a cold immediately after a loved one has passed.

In the early stages of a bereavement, it is normal for your emotional state to fluctuate frequently to the reaction of no longer having your loved one around. It may take time to properly come to the realisation of what has happened and how you can now try to come to terms with having to let them go. There is no right or wrong way to cope with or move on from this experience. What you may be feeling through your own bereavement process will be discussed in more detail in the next two sections.

# My thoughts on 'letting go'...

'When we meet real tragedy in life, we can react in two ways – either by losing hope and falling into self-destructive habits, or by using the challenge to find our inner strength.'

- The Dalai Lama

# The Death of a Parent

It is difficult to endure the loss of a parent. Even though it may be regarded as an inevitable event in our lifetime because often our parents will pass over before us. Losing such a significant person, who not only brought us into this world but also nurtured us until we reached adulthood and beyond, can make you feel vulnerable when they are no longer around.

You may still feel like this, even if your loved one was in the end stages of their dementia prior to their death and your 'caring roles' had become reversed for several years since their illness had progressed.

However, it is important to acknowledge that not everyone may have had the 'perfect' relationship with their parents when they were growing up. If this was you, then you may have felt pressured into providing support for them during their illness. This experience may have strengthened your relationship because a lot of what had gone on in the past may have been forgotten by your loved one or their characteristics that were once a problem to you, may have changed as their dementia progressed. Alternatively, you may have experienced difficult times with your parent both before and during their illness, leaving you with perhaps many unhappy memories and a turmoil of emotions.

Your parent, during their dementia journey, may have inevitably become unrecognisable. This may have been for many different reasons, including significant changes in their behaviour and personality. A lot of their frustrations may have been vented towards you in a verbal or physical way. Such 'bad' times are probably still very clearly remembered and this may be causing you to struggle with how you feel since they have passed away. Coming to terms with losing two very different parents, one before the illness and one after may be causing a conflict of having happy memories prior to the dementia mixed with unhappy experiences during their illness too.

Challenging as it may be, endeavour where possible to reflect on the happy times you both shared. It is also important to recognise that the bad times were the 'illness' and not the fault of your parent.

Another difficult part of the illness to accept, was probably watching your parent's memories disappear as their dementia progressed. This may have included your childhood and adult memories that you once both shared. For example, your first day at school or your wedding day. Some of you may have experienced the tragic situation when your parent began to not recognise who you were or mixed you up with another member of the family. I am often told that many caregivers feel that this is the worst experience that they endure with this illness. If this happened to you, how did you come to terms with this situation at the time?

Dementia often leaves a huge impact on everyone involved and can have heart rendering consequences. Dawn's story below illustrates how difficult things were for her both during and after losing her mum to dementia.

## Dawn's Story

I never thought I could ever lose my beautiful mum and my best friend. At the beginning of my beautiful mum's illness, she would tell stories that I would not understand or talk about events that never happened (unless they were stories from her childhood that we never knew about), but she believed them deeply.

Mum would put things in places where it was hard to find, like her jewellery in saucepans or cups in the kitchen cupboards, also scourers we found in the fridge. The day came while caring for Mum that she forgot how to use the toilet and what to do on the toilet. I was devastated and this was when I realised Mum was really very poorly. I always thought dementia was an old age ailment, I never thought that it was terminal, and I would lose my beautiful mum to this terrible cruel disease.

I gave up my full-time job and cared for her 24/7. When I needed a rest and a break my two sisters would come to stay over at Mum's so I could go to my own family home. Also, my two daughters would help out as much as they could.

I found myself becoming so low and so lost as I had never dealt with anything like this and did not have a clue, but I succeeded and hope I did my very best for my mum. I found myself grieving for my mum while she was with us; it was terrible, in a way I knew she had gone, the mum I knew and loved deeply. There were just little bits left of her.

Mum was a very loving and caring lady but, in her illness, she seemed so angry and could become very aggressive. When I was caring for my mum at home, I introduced her to a doll and doll's clothing because I thought this may be a comfort to her and it was. When she became agitated or frightened, I used the doll to calm her and it seemed to work for a short while.

We used to dance and mess about to the Abba 'Mamma Mia' movie. She loved the film but when it finished, she had forgot she had watched it, so I had to keep putting it on over and over for her. She seemed so happy sitting there watching it as the hours passed by. I would also put dishes on the kitchen side, and she would wash and dry them over and over; she was enjoying keeping busy.

Mum would hallucinate a lot and said several times that there was a little girl standing beside the television. I knew and was aware that the medication she was taking could cause this; if not, I would have believed there was, because she was so convinced that the little girl was there, bless her.

***

I thank Dawn for sharing her story in this book, as I know she wanted her experience to help others in a similar situation. 'Gone But Not Forgotten' is dedicated to Dawn, her sister Debbie and their beloved mum Shirley who died from this terrible illness in 2013. I personally know Dawn and Debbie and met Shirley when she had dementia. The grief they had for the loss of their mum both before and after her illness, brought home to me that there was a need for a book to be written to support others going through a similar journey. With this in mind, I decided to create 'Gone But Not Forgotten'.

## My thoughts on 'losing' my parent during the time of their dementia illness...

# Further thoughts since my parent has passed away...

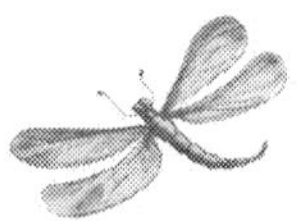

# The Death of a Spouse

If it was your husband, wife or partner that had dementia then I am sure this will have had a profound effect on your relationship. You may have perhaps felt like you had lost your 'soul mate' during their dementia journey when treasured memories you shared could no longer be retrieved and plans for your future destroyed. Similarly, to what has been previously written on losing a parent to dementia, you may have gone through a rollercoaster of emotions and stages. This may have caused you to experience a more 'parent and child' partnership as their dementia progressed, especially if your spouse was dependent upon you to help them with their basic needs.

Your spouse's personality may have completely changed during their illness causing them to be a very different person to the one you fell in love with. You may have struggled to recognise them at times and become frustrated with how their dementia had damaged your partnership.

Perhaps your loved one needed to go into a long-term care home. This may have been the first time in years that you had spent time apart. It may have left you living on your own, re-evaluating your finances, sorting out legalities and doing all the household chores and jobs by yourself.

## My thoughts on 'losing' my spouse during the time of their dementia illness...

# Further thoughts since my spouse has passed away...

# The Death of a Child

Younger people being diagnosed with dementia is being more frequently recognised and discussed. It must therefore be acknowledged that there may be some of you reading this book that have been affected by the death of a child or younger person to dementia.

It is widely reported that people are now living longer. This also gives rise to more parents out-living their children and children being diagnosed with dementia is no exception to this.

I can recall several years ago going to a Care Show, where an elderly lady had been asked to go up on stage and speak about her personal experiences with dementia. The audience quickly became shocked when they realised that she was talking about her own daughter having the illness. She explained how she had made a very difficult decision to move her daughter into a care home, as she now felt unable to cope with looking after her at home.

In the future, this could become more of a reality for parents, especially with a rise in people being diagnosed with 'young onset dementia', like frontotemporal dementia, which can affect people in their 30s, 40s, 50s and 60s.

If you have been a parent affected by dementia, you may have found yourself re-living your parenting role due to your child's illness.

Losing your child or a younger relative after their dementia, may have conjured up a multitude of feelings including the injustice of losing someone so young and to such a cruel illness.

## My thoughts on 'losing' my child during the time of their dementia illness...

## Further thoughts since my child has passed away...

# The Death of a Relative Or Friend

You may have not been personally affected by any of the above but instead experienced dementia and loss with another close relative like a grandparent, brother, sister, uncle, auntie or even a close friend.

There may have been similarities to the experiences already mentioned when previously discussing a parent, spouse and child. Space is left below for you to write any thoughts about losing this special person in your life.

## My thoughts on losing __________ during the time of their dementia illness...

______________________________________________

______________________________________________

______________________________________________

______________________________________________

______________________________________________

______________________________________________

Further thoughts since __________ has passed away...

*'Those we love don't go away,*

*They walk beside us every day,*

*Unseen, unheard, but always near,*

*Still loved, still missed and very dear.'*

~ Author Unknown

# The Funeral

A funeral is a time not only to celebrate their life but also to reflect upon your personal memories and an opportunity to say your final goodbyes. The funeral of your loved one was possibly either a burial or a cremation. The type of service you had may have been determined by their cultural or religious beliefs.

Hopefully the organising of the funeral went smoothly in accordance with your loved one's wishes, with family and friends around you to offer condolences and support. Your loved one may have already discussed funeral arrangements before their illness, like their choice of hymns or songs, the type of flowers they would like and where the wake would be held afterwards.

Although a funeral is often dreaded, there may have been things that happened during the day that have since been a comfort to you. For instance, the words expressed by the person conducting the service, the money raised for your chosen charity or the love and support from those who attended.

# Thoughts about my loved one's funeral...

# The Grief That Follows...

Grief can conjure up a mixture of emotions and often no two days will feel the same. There will be times when you feel like you are starting to move on, only to then have a day that you struggle to get through. Such days may make you feel like you have taken a step backwards rather than forward in your grieving process.

Special events in your life can trigger you to feel more upset that your loved one is no longer around, like a wedding or the birth of a baby in your family.

A lot of people will say that the first year of losing your loved one can be the most challenging because it is a time when you face the first Christmas, birthday or for example, anniversary without them.

Something as simple as a familiar piece of music playing on the radio or a favourite place that you both once visited may cause you to suddenly feel emotional.

Don't feel despondent if your bereavement still feels 'raw' weeks and even months after your loved one has passed away. There is no magic timescale. It is, however, essential that you don't suffer in silence. Seek professional help if you feel your bereavement or escalating low moods are becoming worse or more difficult to cope with.

It is important to let go of any emotions. So, don't try to 'bottle things up' as crying is a normal reaction to a loss. Men will often try to avoid showing how upset they are, especially in front of others. This may be often due to old fashioned beliefs that 'men don't cry' and that they must always keep a 'stiff upper lip' in times of sadness. However, it is acceptable to release emotion through crying regardless of whether you are male or female. You may prefer to choose an appropriate time or place that feels right for you. Perhaps when you are alone or with people that you feel 'comfortable' with.

Grief is an individual thing. So, try not to compare yourself to others. Take each day at a time. There is no set pattern to follow, so just because other people in your family seem to be coping better than you, this may not be necessarily the case.

A bereavement can conjure up a mixture of feelings, many of which are discussed in more detail in subsequent sections of this book. It is normal to find yourself moving from one emotion to another, which is why grief often has a 'rollercoaster' effect on your life.

## Your thoughts on what has been discussed above...

*'Some people come into our lives,
leave footprints on our hearts, and we
are never the same.'*

~ Author Unknown

# Physical Effects of Loss

Taking care of your own health may have been a low priority, while your loved one was still living and even during your bereavement too. However, it is essential that you do look after yourself, as you don't want ill health adding to any stress that is already in your life. I am also sure that your loved one would not wish for you to be unwell, along with other family members who may still depend on you being fit and active, especially if you still have a young family or an aging parent that relies on your support.

During your bereavement you may have experienced a loss of appetite or a lack of motivation to cook. You may have started to rely on 'picking' at food, eating ready meals, buying take-aways or having unhealthy snacks. Maybe you have started to take comfort from food and eating to enhance your mood. If you are gaining extra weight it can in time start to have a detrimental effect on your health. A poor diet could lead to a deficiency in essential vitamins and minerals that can lead to depression, poor concentration, and mood swings. An unhealthy lifestyle can also lead to a lower immunity leaving you susceptible to coughs, colds and sickness bugs and in the long-term cause obesity increasing your risk of strokes and heart problems.

Maintaining good physical health will also rely upon regular exercise. Try to get out into the fresh air for at least 30 minutes a day. Having a daily walk is an excellent way to exercise, as well as an opportunity to 'clear your head' if required. You may currently feel reluctant to join an exercise class, enrol in a gym or take up swimming, however in time these activities may help you to re-focus your life, as well as give an opportunity to meet new people and increase your own natural 'feel good' hormones called endorphins.

It is reasonable to expect that if you smoke or continually exceed the recommended weekly alcohol units, this may start to cause you serious health problems in the future. During the initial time of bereavement, and through your dementia journey, they may have played a big part in helping you to relax, however, moving forward you may want to consider the impact that long term use will have.

Experiencing fatigue is not uncommon and you may find it difficult to get proper rest and sleep. You may also be suffering from more aches and pains which could be due to tension or anxiety. Ensure you incorporate as many things as possible that help you to relax, for instance, listening to calming music, having a milky drink before bedtime, reading a book or having a relaxing soak in the bath.

## Thoughts I have regarding my physical wellbeing...

## Actions I can take to improve my physical wellbeing are...

1) ______________________________________________

______________________________________________

______________________________________________

2) ______________________________________________

______________________________________________

______________________________________________

3) ______________________________________________

______________________________________________

______________________________________________

4) ______________________________________________

______________________________________________

______________________________________________

5) ______________________________________________

______________________________________________

______________________________________________

*'Perhaps this is what the stories meant when they called somebody heartsick. Your heart and your stomach and your whole insides felt empty and hollow and aching.'*

~ Gabriel Garcia Marquez

# Psychological Effects of Loss

When people think about bereavement, they often focus on the psychological impact of it. Kübler-Ross has written a lot about the different stages of grief which will be discussed in more detail in Section 2.

Your bereavement journey will be unique to you. It can't be compared to other people, because we are all different in how we deal with our own grief. Your loved one would still want you to 'live' your life, as I am sure you would want the same for them, if it had been the other way around. However, at times you may understandably feel that this is easier said than done.

Take your bereavement journey a day at a time. Remember the good times with a smile and try to rationalise, where you can, on the more 'difficult' times caused by their dementia illness.

The psychological effects related to a dementia bereavement is a vast subject which will be discussed further throughout this book.

Never struggle alone with your grief; seek medical advice if you really think you are unable to move on with your life.

## Thoughts I have about my psychological wellbeing...

# Actions I can take to improve my psychological wellbeing are...

1) ________________________________________

________________________________________

________________________________________

2) ________________________________________

________________________________________

________________________________________

3) ________________________________________

________________________________________

________________________________________

4) ________________________________________

________________________________________

________________________________________

5) ________________________________________

________________________________________

________________________________________

# Social Effects of Loss

In the immediate days after your loved one's death you may have been overwhelmed with the number of cards, phone calls and visits. However, you may now feel quite alone when faced with getting on with your own life again.

There have possibly been many changes to your social circumstances during your dementia journey. Friends and relatives may have 'drifted' away from you, when you and your loved one were living with their dementia. This may have been for a variety of reasons, for example, you may have been unable to go out and socialise, your friends may have struggled to come to terms with your loved one having dementia or perhaps both of your lives became busier.

You may now want to re-kindle old friendships or alternatively make new friends by joining a group or club that interests you. Many of us feel quite lonely if we don't have people around us. Having an active social life may be just the boost that you require.

Perhaps you had to give up a job to look after your loved one and are now faced with the decision around whether to work again. If you are still working age or you need to return to work for financial reasons, try to find work that you have done before or a job that interests you.

If you are now retired or unable to work and are financially struggling, make enquires at your local Citizens Advice Bureau, financial advisor, internet or social services as to whether you could be entitled to any benefits.

## Thoughts I have about my social wellbeing...

## Actions I can take to improve my social wellbeing are...

1) ____________________________________________

____________________________________________

____________________________________________

2) ____________________________________________

____________________________________________

____________________________________________

3) ____________________________________________

____________________________________________

____________________________________________

4) ____________________________________________

____________________________________________

____________________________________________

5) ____________________________________________

____________________________________________

____________________________________________

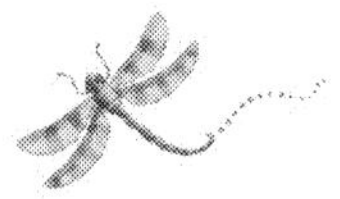

*'In this sad world of ours sorrow comes to all and it often comes with bitter agony. Perfect relief is not possible except with time. You cannot now believe that you will ever feel better. But this is not true. You are sure to be happy again. Knowing this, truly believing it, will make you less miserable now. I have had enough experience to make this statement.'*

~ Abraham Lincoln

# Spiritual Effects Of Loss

I acknowledge that spirituality is not for everyone and it very much depends upon your own beliefs. Having a religion, spending time in nature or doing some 'natural' healing like reiki or meditation are just some forms of spirituality, that may help you to move forward with your loss.

If you have a religious belief it may help you to attend your local church service or talk to your vicar or priest. Having an involvement with a church community, regularly saying prayers, reading Bible psalms or singing hymns, could become a valuable support and comfort to you.

# Examples of Hymns

## The Day Thou Gavest Lord Has Ended

(uplifting hymn rather than a sorrowful one sung at funerals)

The day Thou gavest, Lord, is ended,
The darkness falls at Thy behest;
To Thee our morning Hymns ascended,
Thy praise shall sanctify our rest.

We thank Thee that Thy church, unsleeping,
While earth rolls onward into light,
Through all the world her watch is keeping,
And rests not now by day or night.

As over each continent and island
The dawn leads on another day,
The voice of prayer is never silent,
Nor dies the strain of praise away.

The sun that bids us rest is waking
Our brethren 'neath the western sky,
And hour by hour fresh lips are making
Thy wondrous doings heard on high.

So be it, Lord; Thy throne shall never
Like Earth's proud empires, pass away:
Thy kingdom stands, and grows forever,
Till all Thy creatures own Thy sway.

## Amazing Grace

(about finding peace after death)

Amazing Grace, How sweet the sound
That saved a wretch like me
I once was lost, but now am found
T'was blind but now I see.

T'was Grace that taught my heart to fear
And Grace, my fears relieved
How precious did that grace appear
The hour I first believed.

Through many dangers, toils and snares
We have already come.
T'was grace that brought us safe thus far
And grace will lead us home.

## Abide With Me

(hymn asking God for support and help)

Abide with me:
Fast falls the even tide;
The darkness deepens:
Lord, with me abide!
When other helpers fail,
And comforts flee,
Help of the helpless,

O abide with me!
Swift to its close
Ebbs out life's little day;
Earth's joys grow dim;
Its glories pass away;
Change and decay in all
Around I see;
O Thou who changest
Not, abide with me!

I need Thy presence
Ev'ry passing hour:

What but Thy grace can
Foil the tempter's pow'r?
Who like Thyself my guide
And stay can be?
Through cloud and sunshine,
O abide with me!

## The Lord Is My Shepherd (Psalm 23)

(uplifting hymn offering guidance)

The Lord's my Shepherd, I'll not want;
He makes me down to lie
In pastures green; He leadeth me
The quiet waters by.

My soul He doth restore again,
And me to walk doth make
Within the paths of righteousness,
E'en for His own name's sake.

Yea, though I walk in death's dark vale,
Yet will I fear no ill;

For Thou art with me, and Thy rod
And staff my comfort still.

My table Thou hast furnished me
In presence of my foes;
My head Thou dost with oil anoint,
And my cup overflows.

Goodness and mercy all my life
Shall surely follow me;
And in God's house forevermore,
My dwelling place shall be.

# Examples of Psalms

I waited patiently for the LORD,
He turned to me and heard my cry.
He lifted me out of the slimy pit, out of the mud and mire;
He set my feet on a rock and gave me a firm place to stand.
He put a new song in my mouth, a hymn of praise to our God.
Many will see and fear and put their trust in the LORD.
Blessed is the man who makes the LORD his trust, who does not look to the proud, to those who turn aside to false gods.

~ Psalm 40:1-4 NIV ~

Whenever I am afraid, I will trust in You.

~ Psalm 56:3 ~

My comfort in my suffering is this:
Your promise preserves my life.

~ Psalm 119:50 ~

Spiritual practices like reiki and meditation can be relaxing and therapeutic. Reiki is a wonderful healing treatment. There will be local qualified practitioners in your area or alternatively you may like to learn how to do reiki on yourself. If meditation interests you, purchasing CDs or downloading some techniques will provide you with a beginner's guide on how to do it.

A basic meditation technique to get you started simply involves taking a slow deep breath in and then out, while clearing your mind of any thoughts that may start to creep in. Build the time up gradually that you do this, as initially you may find it hard to focus for more than a couple of minutes.

Spirituality does not need to involve religion or relaxation therapies, just going outside and walking in nature may give you a sense of calmness in order to clear your mind. Taking in the sights, sounds and smells around you will help you to relax.

For some, visiting a spiritualist church or going to a reputable spiritualist or medium will be a great source of comfort. Others may disagree with this concept and feel it has no place in their life.

Lynn Robinson has written a book 'A Light To Guide Us Home' which is about her experiences of discovering her gift as a medium. She has helped many people during their loss. She talks below about her 'gift' and how it has helped people in times of bereavement, as well as receiving messages from people who have dementia and other life changing illnesses.

## Do not worry, I am here

When I wrote my book 'A Light To Guide Us Home', I wrote about a meeting I had with an author called Pam. We had planned to meet as she was going to give me some marketing tips about my new book, or so I thought. Let me introduce myself, I am Lynn Robinson, I am a medium and energy healer, and nothing in my world is ever as it seems. During my meeting with Pam, I realised that I was there to bring her some comfort and not to gain tips about publishing my book.

You see, her mother-in-law had late stages of Alzheimer's, and they visited her every day as she was in a nursing home. The visits were becoming more and more upsetting, as she didn't recognise them at all. This caused distress to them all including her mother-in-law. She would get upset and was worried that strangers were around her. Without a doubt, this created some very upsetting moments indeed, but during my visit to see Pam a strange thing happened. Pam asked would I see if I could pick up any of her loved ones. She had brought some items of jewellery for me to hold, you see when I do this I can pick up the energy of the person to whom it belonged.

The energy of a lady came to me and began to talk with me. I was passing messages to Pam; the messages were not like other messages I have had for clients, the lady seemed to drift in and out, and I couldn't seem to keep a hold on the energy. I apologised to Pam and told her that this doesn't usually happen, once the spirit of a loved one comes in, they stay until I have finished.

Pam sat opposite me and said very little; there were three of us at this meeting. My friend Bev had introduced me to Pam and had taken the journey with me. While I had been talking to Pam, Bev had been outside taking a telephone call; on her return she heard me talking about the lady in question. When she heard me mention that I thought the lady had Alzheimer's she looked over to Pam quite upset and said, "Oh lovely, I am sorry I didn't know she had died."

The next words out of Pam's mouth shocked us all: "She hasn't," she said looking at me with her eyes wide open. I then realised why I couldn't keep hold of her energy, this was the beginning of an amazing journey for me, and this was why I had to meet Pam. The energy of the lady came close to me again, and the words were clear: 'Please don't stop, please don't stop'. "I am sorry, I don't understand the message," I told Pam.

Pam looked at me and told me that she did understand. she explained how they had sat this very day with their mother; she was particularly agitated this morning, and they had all got very upset. Pam's husband had decided to visit less often, just go a couple of times a week instead of every day, as this was becoming more and more painful every visit. His mother had heard this, you see, and she didn't want them to stop visiting. We were all quite shocked at the possibility of a soul that was still inside of a living body could come and pass a message to me.

On my return home I decided to consult my guides and ask them how this was possible. My guides are lovely, and they have helped me to understand my job here many times over the years.

They began to explain to me the different stages of dementia and Alzheimer's, each one as painful for the family and the host. They also talked in great detail of other illnesses that seem to take your loved one away sometimes for long periods of time. With most terminal diseases there are periods of time when your loved one just looks as if they are not there. I sat with my own father and watched this happen as he passed with cancer. My guides explained what was happening during this time; they told me that the human body, the solid skin and bone, is what was dying and that your soul never dies. Many times during the illness the soul will need relief from the body, and so will be lifted out and allowed to be free for periods of time. Sometimes the soul will stay, in the same room; sometimes the soul will leave and go on a journey, to visit loved ones both at home and in heaven.

I was amazed at what I was hearing, and everything that had happened to me at the meeting with Pam became apparent. They told me of how the brain kept the body going, and that the soul was a completely different part of the host, the soul was pure and beautiful and could never be dented or damaged by illness. As the human body went through the stages of a disease, not just mental illness, the soul would always release at some time and gain its energy.

I found all this fascinating, and I thought of how much comfort this would bring to many people who sat day in and day out worrying about their loved ones deteriorating in their hospital beds. I asked my guides why they had shown me this, and why I was sent to Pam.

I heard a giggle. "You will see," they answered.

It wasn't long before all became apparent; people started to come to me for readings, people who were suffering while their loved ones seemed to be lost in the dreadful state of not knowing who they were.

These people had been guided to me so that I could tune into their loved ones and pass messages to them of love and gratitude for all they were doing or all they had done. I have met many people since my meeting with Pam, and they have all received beautiful and comforting messages from their loved ones, both still in the land of the living and those who have passed over. I must tell you that this part of my work has been so very satisfying, just to bring such fantastic comfort to those who are distraught by what these life-changing illnesses cause.

I feel the message to all who are reading this, and know exactly how this feels, to talk to them as if they are still there, talk about all the things you would have talked about when they were well. Act as if there is nothing wrong; I promise you this, they are there, they are listening and during the quiet times and the times when they look so vacant, know that their beautiful soul is just beside you, holding your heart in their hands and trying to help you to feel some peace yourself.

There are many things in life and death that we cannot explain, and the scientist in us will look for the logic, but that is your brain, your brain is programmed to do this. But please remember that just because we cannot see it doesn't mean that it does not exist, we cannot see the air, but yet we take deep breaths, we cannot understand gravity, yet we trust that it is there. Our souls are here for just a while, just until it is time for us to go back to the source energy, the energy from which we were created.

There are no limits to what your soul is capable of, and I thank the soul of Pam's mother-in-law for helping me to understand just how incredible the unknown is.

In my book, Angels Around Us, I have written about many journeys I have taken over the years and the many clients who have received a miracle during their readings.

Please take peace from knowing that as you read this, right this very moment, the soul of a loved one is at your side. Close your eyes for one minute and say hello, they have come to bring you comfort and love.

*Lynn Robinson*

www.lynn-robinson-medium.co.uk

## Thoughts I have about my spiritual wellbeing...

# Actions I can take to improve my spiritual wellbeing are…

1) ______________________________

______________________________

______________________________

2) ______________________________

______________________________

______________________________

3) ______________________________

______________________________

______________________________

4) ______________________________

______________________________

______________________________

5) ______________________________

______________________________

______________________________

# Further Thoughts

# SECTION 2

## Stages of Bereavement

### *Do Not Stand at My Grave and Weep*

*Do not stand at my grave and weep.*
*I am not there.*
*I do not sleep.*
*I am a thousand winds that blow.*
*I am the diamond glints on snow.*
*I am the sunlight on ripened grain.*
*I am the gentle autumn's rain.*
*When you awaken in the morning's hush,*
*I am the swift uplifting rush*
*Of quiet birds in circled flight.*
*I am the soft stars that shine at night.*
*Do not stand at my grave and cry;*
*I am not there.*
*I did not die.*

~ Mary Frye

# Stages of Bereavement

There are many theories about grief, one of the most famous is by Swiss psychiatrist Elizabeth Kübler-Ross who identified five main stages:

**Denial**

**Anger**

**Bargaining**

**Depression**

**Acceptance**

Kübler-Ross stated that most people during a time of grief will experience at least two out of these five stages. She also acknowledged that a lot of us will re-visit or even go on to experience a new stage at any time following a loved one's death, even if this is years later. Your own bereavement is personal to you, therefore, the order of the stages and the time spent on them will also be an individual process too.

Denial, anger, bargaining, depression, and acceptance will be discussed in more detail in this section. Each area and how it may relate to you during your time of personal grief will be analysed as you may have possibly already faced some, if not all these stages during your loved one's dementia journey, and since they have passed away too. You may have also experienced other emotions during your bereavement, some of these will also be discussed after Kübler-Ross's five stages.

Grief is not like an illness that we can recover from, it often remains with us throughout our life. How we cope with it and the emotions we experience may vary at different times. When we lose someone close it is inevitable that our life will change and our loss will challenge us. The feelings connected with not having them around may remain, however it's important that you can find ways to move forward and continue to 'live' your life in the best way possible.

# DENIAL

Even if the death of your loved one was expected, it is not unusual that the reality of no longer having them around is still hard to accept. You may be experiencing feelings of numbness and disbelief which is a normal and common reaction to have.

The dementia journey that you both endured may still feel quite 'raw'. Coming to terms with the often-marked changes in your loved one's behaviour, personality and the cruel end stages may still be having an impact on you. Your loved one's illness may have gone on for many years, but you may still feel some denial around how the illness affected them, as well as the fact that they are no longer here.

You may now be left wondering how you can move forward with your own life, especially if your life for many years revolved around their illness. For instance, you may have looked after your loved one full time at home and got used to the visits from carers and other professionals supporting you in the community. Alternatively, your loved one may have been in a care home which you may have regarded as your 'second home' due to visiting your loved one regularly and making friends with the staff, residents and fellow visitors. Moving on after a familiar routine and the people involved, may have also had a profound effect on you.

In the small care home where I work the families and staff become one big 'family' unit so inevitably when we lose someone, a sense of loss is felt by everyone.

As previously discussed in the last section, perhaps your loved one despite having dementia may have died quite suddenly from another chronic illness or sudden onset of a fatal illness like a heart attack or stroke. Their sudden death from an illness unrelated to their dementia may have left you feeling even more denial or disbelief due to them passing away more quickly than you had anticipated.

Experiencing denial as part of the bereavement process is often a coping mechanism, as it helps you to set a 'pace' for your own grief. It can help you to come to terms and adjust to your loss in your own time, rather than it 'hitting you like a sledgehammer' causing it to have a huge emotional impact which could lead to an inability to move forward with your own life.

Once you start to adapt and move on from this stage of denial, the rest of your healing process can start to begin.

## My thoughts on denial...

# ANGER

Anger can be conjured up for a variety of reasons both during and after your loved one's illness. However, it is important to recognise that holding on to prolonged feelings of anger can have a progressively harmful effect on you as you try to move forward in your own life.

Moving away from such negative feelings will depend upon why you are feeling angry in the first place. Such feelings may have been triggered when reflecting on what has gone on in the past, as well as how you now feel at this moment in time. Living with anger may provoke thoughts like…

Why me?

Why did my love one die in this way?

They did not deserve this.

I should have had many more years with them.

Who can I blame?

This could be playing a big part as to why you are now feeling angry. You may blame yourself, other members of your family or the professionals involved in your loved one's care for the events during their illness or leading up to their death.

This 'blame' reaction may cause you to vent anger towards yourself or aim it towards others. If you have a religious faith you may start to question if there really is a 'God' as you reflect on how unfair life has been for you and your loved one.

If you are feeling angry, this needs to be acknowledged but at the same time released, in a controlled and safe manner. For instance, by thumping a cushion or screaming and shouting out loud when you are alone. Holding on to pent up feelings of anger and not allowing such emotions to be set free can build up to such a point that you may risk venting them inappropriately or without control.

Although we may not be able to undo what has gone on in the past, we may feel better if something positive is gained from a negative situation that you found yourself in. For example, if anger is stemmed from the frustration that your loved one's end-of-life care was not carried out to an acceptable standard, then raise an official complaint with the organisation concerned, as this may prevent similar mistakes happening to other families in the future.

If you are experiencing feelings of anger towards a member of your own family, acknowledge that although you still regarded their actions as inappropriate, holding on to these emotions in the long term will only have a detrimental effect on your own wellbeing.

It is essential to let any angry feelings go, so you can naturally heal and move forward with your own life.

## My thoughts on anger…

# Bargaining

You may have found yourself 'bargaining' a lot during your loved one's dementia illness. For example, when your loved one refused to eat you may have willed them to just have one decent meal a day to prevent them from becoming too frail or if your loved one was often restless at night you may have wished for them to have just one peaceful night sleep each week so that you too, could have some much needed rest to help you cope with the daily challenges ahead.

You may have also experienced this stage since the death of your loved one, as this emotion is often part of our grieving process too. For instance, you may have found yourself wishing that you could spend just one hour with your loved one because you miss them so much. Or if your loved one was younger than you, you may have thought that it should have been you dying first and not them.

'Bargaining' during your bereavement process, may also relate to the need to make changes with the current situation before you can move on. For example, you may feel that you are unable to progress with your grief until you can move to a new house because your current location is a constant reminder of your loved one and past events. Or alternatively, you may desire to be kept busy because this distracts you from facing up to how you are feeling.

Once you begin to 'accept' past and present events as part of your adjustment to how your life is now, moving forward will become an easier transition.

## My thoughts on bargaining...

# Depression

Depression is an accepted, frequently visited and widely acknowledged stage of grief. It is reasonable to anticipate that most people will experience this at some time, if not immediately after their loved one's death.

The realisation of no longer seeing and spending time with the one you love may have now become more of a reality. As time progresses following their death, you may have already gone through episodes of extreme low moods, where you have felt like running away and hiding from everything around you.

Depression can cause a downward spiral of uncontrolled emotions, which can have a profound effect on you moving on and coming to terms with the death of your loved one. During such times you may find yourself wanting to withdraw from everyday life and often feel like you view the world through a foggy haze. It may be difficult to eat due to a lack of appetite or struggle to switch off when going to sleep.

If possible, seek support from others during these times, whether this is family members or valued friends. If you go beyond the 'normal' feelings of depression related to your bereavement, for example, you frequently struggle to function on a daily basis or have suicidal thoughts, then I urge you to immediately seek professional help that can provide you with more specialised support.

## My thoughts on depression…

# ACCEPTANCE

The 'acceptance' stage of bereavement does not mean that you have moved on from your loved one's death, it is an acknowledgement that you are now coming to terms with your loss by starting to re-build your own life as best you can. Your loved one will never be forgotten but as time progresses you will inevitably accept that you must cope and 'live' without them.

Take comfort when you gain a realisation that your life will be ok and value the supportive network of family and friends around you. It is normal to go through an evolving cycle of adjustment and re-adjustment as you experience good and bad days. Eventually the good days will start to outweigh the bad ones...just give yourself time.

There may be occasions when you encounter a succession of challenging days; these may arrive unexpectedly and cause a mixture of negative emotions. If this happens, avoid dwelling too much on it, our grief can often feel like a rollercoaster. Instead remember to take each day as it comes and don't pressurise yourself into thinking that you should live every day like nothing has happened.

It is completely natural to experience more intense grief on 'memorable days' like birthdays, Christmas and anniversaries. It is important to accept that such days will be more difficult. Suggestions on how to cope better during these times will be discussed in more detail in Section 4.

## My thoughts on acceptance…

*'The most beautiful people we have known are those who have known defeat, known suffering, known struggle, known loss, and have found their way out of the depths.'*

~ Dr Elisabeth Kübler-Ross

# Other Emotions Experienced

During your bereavement process, you may have experienced a variety of other emotions, as well as Kübler-Ross's five stages that have already been discussed. These may have had or could still be having a major influence on your day-to-day living. At times it will feel that you are 'stuck' on a certain emotion which is preventing you from moving forward.

Listed below are some emotions that may resonate with you, along with examples on how they may be having an impact on your life. There is space below for you to write any thoughts you may have on each one.

**Shock** - can often occur when your loved one passes away unexpectedly, possibly due to an unrelated or underlying illness. The shock of this sudden death may be difficult for you to adjust to and come to terms with initially. Perhaps you struggled to accept that they had died or were unable to have an opportunity to say your final goodbyes while they were living.

# My thoughts on shock...

**Relief** - can be felt by relatives after a chronic and drawn out illness like dementia. You may now feel relieved that your loved one is no longer suffering. Their dementia would have probably been a difficult journey and so experiencing relief may trigger a mixture of emotions, leaving you wondering whether it is appropriate for you to be feeling this way. Don't feel guilty, your relief is with the end of their illness and not with losing the person you love.

## My thoughts on relief...

**Emotional pain** – could be described as chronic, physical pain experienced when going through a bereavement, often caused by tension or rigidity during times of anxiety and heightened periods of emotion. It can lead to headaches and painful muscles and joints. You may have heard people talk about 'enduring the pain' of a highly stressful situation; bereavement is just one example of this.

## My thoughts on emotional pain…

**Frustration** - is a widely recognised emotion for dementia caregivers and can be felt for a variety of reasons. You may still feel frustrated that your loved one was taken prematurely to dementia, which had a major impact on plans you had made for the future. Alternatively, you may be frustrated over financial issues you have had to deal with since they have passed over.

## My thoughts on frustration...

**Anxiety** – may feel like an ongoing emotion in your life, experienced not only during your bereavement but probably since your loved one was first diagnosed with dementia. Feelings of anxiety may be related to coping with the re-building of your life without your loved one around or it may be in relation to having to sell their property or sort out legal matters following their death.

## My thoughts on anxiety…

**Avoidance** - of certain situations or people may be a frequent occurrence since your loved one has passed away. You may have accepted this initially, however as time progresses the realisation that certain things need to be faced up to may be causing you a build-up of stress. For instance, you may be avoiding the task of sorting through your loved one's belongings or putting off going back to work.

## My thoughts on avoidance...

**Afraid** - of what the future may hold or how other members of your family will cope following your loved one's death, may now be having a detrimental effect on you. Perhaps, you are now left wondering how your own life can ever be 'normal' again, especially, if your loved one's illness has left you and your family with a lot of bad experiences and memories.

## My thoughts on being afraid...

**Overwhelm** - may have been an ongoing emotion that you have felt since your loved one's dementia progressed. You may at times reflect back on the amount of 'sorting out' you have had to do both during and after their illness. For example finding long term care establishments, organising their health and financial needs and since passing away, organising their funeral and informing relevant personnel about their death.

## My thoughts on overwhelm...

**Hostility** – could have been vented towards other members of your family or the dementia illness that robbed you of your loved one. Perhaps you have had disagreements with your family, both before and after the death of your loved one. For instance, you may not have agreed on how they were being looked after or experienced arguments about the funeral arrangements taking place. Alternatively, you may still feel hostile towards the dementia illness and how it caused your loved one to slip away from the person you once knew.

## My thoughts on hostility…

**Distraught** - feelings may have caused you to have prolonged periods of upset both during and after your dementia journey. This type of intense reaction illustrates the scale of impact that dementia can have on all those involved. You may have felt distraught about how dementia had changed your loved one both physically and psychologically or how your loved one had lingered with the end stages of their illness.

## My thoughts on feeling distraught...

**Sadness** - is probably one of the most frequent emotions experienced during a bereavement. Feeling sad, especially during the early stages of losing someone is a natural reaction to your loss. Such feelings may be felt as soon as you wake up and realise your loved one is no longer with you or when you hear a piece of music that reminds you of them.

## My thoughts on sadness...

**Guilty** - feelings may have stayed with you since your loved one's death. Perhaps you still feel guilty about putting them into a long-term care setting when you were no longer able to look after them. You may also feel guilty about not visiting them as much as you would have liked because you did not know how to respond and cope with their illness.

## My thoughts on feeling guilty...

**Dread** - of certain situations may be having an impact on you. For example, perhaps you need to financially go back to work after years of being your loved one's carer or returning to an 'empty' house that doesn't feel the same since your loved one has gone. Having now experienced dementia, you may now dread the illness occurring again in the future, with another member of your family.

## My thoughts on facing dread...

**Envy** - may be directed towards those that you know that still have their 'loved one' living. They may be making exciting plans for the future, whereas you are now unfortunately unable to do this with your own family member. Perhaps you are envious that those closest to you are starting to come to terms with their loss, when you are still struggling to move on with yours.

## My thoughts on envy...

**Regretful** - feelings may be centred around situations that occurred during your loved one's illness. Maybe you said things to them out of frustration or anger that you now regret. Alternatively, you may now feel regretful that they did not live to see their milestone birthday or anniversary or be part of a special occasion like a wedding or birth.

## My thoughts on feeling regretful...

**Ashamed** - you may feel like this when you recall how you avoided taking your loved one out for fear that they may 'show you up' in a public place, especially if they would at times become 'vocal' or drop drink or food on the floor. Perhaps you did not like talking about your loved one to people who did not know your circumstances in case you felt 'alienated' by them.

## My thoughts on feeling ashamed...

**Distress** – could be how you are feeling as you revisit situations both before and after your loved one's illness. It could be the first time you have experienced such a close bereavement in your family. It may feel like a very distressing time for you as you try to come to terms with everything that has happened.

## My thoughts on feeling distressed...

**Loss of purpose** - may be felt, especially if you have been the main caregiver for your loved one for many years. 'Losing' this role, as well as your loved one could be now leaving a major void in your life. You may now be left wondering what to do with your life especially if you do not work or are now retired.

## My thoughts on loss of purpose...

*'Everyone grieves in different ways. For some, it could take longer or shorter. I do know it never disappears. An ember still smoulders inside me. Most days, I don't notice it, but, out of the blue, it'll flare to life.'*

~ Maria V Snyder

There may be many other emotions that you may be feeling as you go through your bereavement. There is space below, to write about those that have not already been discussed.

## Other emotions that I may be feeling…

1) ______________________________

## My thoughts on ______________

2) ______________

## My thoughts on ______________

*'Life is eternal, and love is immortal, and death is only a horizon; and a horizon is nothing save the limit of our sight.'*

~ Rossiter Worthington Raymond

As time progresses you may start to feel better for longer periods of time. The loss of your loved one will never go away, as it will always be a significant event in your life. However, accepting what has happened and moving on with your own life may start to become easier.

Endeavour where possible to live in the present, be kind to yourself and take each day at a time. Try where possible to focus on the good memories as I am sure your loved one would wish for you to do this. Setbacks may still occur and there could be times when you feel more sad or anxious. This is all part of the bereavement process and is completely normal. Allow yourself time to heal and don't be too hard on yourself.

You may have been left with not only coping with your own bereavement but also having to support other members of your family with theirs too. For instance, you may have another parent to look after or need to comfort your own children during this time.

Alternatively, you may have feelings of detachment or anger towards those closest around you. This may be centred around them having little understanding about how you are feeling or may criticise you for not being able to pick up the pieces of your life and move on. Avoid comparing your bereavement with others and be upfront with your own feelings because bottling things up or keeping a 'stiff upper lip' will not help you in the long term to move on.

If you have any pro-longed concerns about your own well-being or any other members of your own family, seek advice and help from your GP or local bereavement services.

Your initial thoughts may be that counselling is not for you. However, I urge you to not dismiss it without careful consideration. A trained counsellor is experienced in dealing with a variety of bereavement issues. They will be aware that clients often find sessions emotional and have difficulty at times 'opening up' about their feelings. If you still feel uncomfortable after several counselling sessions, discuss your concerns with the organisation involved, as many solutions may be offered including a change of counsellor. Be mindful that there is sometimes several weeks of waiting time for counselling, unless you decide to go private.

An alternative to counselling could be joining a bereavement support group. If there are not any in your area, then look for an online support group that you could join. More on this in Section 4.

If it feels appropriate and comfortable to you, accept when support is offered by family and friends. A friendly face, a listening ear or a shoulder to cry on may be all you need to clear what is on your mind. Don't think you are putting people out; they are often happy to do something to help and I'm sure you would offer the same support if the situation was reversed.

Fortunately, there is now starting to be less of a stigma about 'opening up' and admitting to mental health issues and a need to seek help. This has been backed by the media and celebrities coming forward to discuss their own mental health issues.

If you are still feeling isolated or unable to turn to others, remember you are never alone in your grief; use this book or a plain journal to vent any frustrations, negative emotions or feelings you are currently experiencing. Finally, and most importantly give yourself time to heal and come to terms with your loss.

## Further Thoughts

___

___

___

# SECTION 3

## Moving Forward from Past Events

### Death Is Nothing At All

*Death is nothing at all.*
*I have only slipped away into the next room.*
*I am I and you are you.*
*Whatever we were to each other,*
*That we are still.*
*Call me by my old familiar name.*
*Speak to me in the easy way you always used.*
*Put no difference into your tone.*
*Wear no forced air of solemnity or sorrow.*
*Laugh as we always laughed,*
*At the little jokes we always enjoyed together.*
*Play, smile, think of me, pray for me.*

*Let my name be ever the household word that it always was.*
*Let it be spoken without effort,*
*Without the ghost of a shadow in it.*
*Life means all that it ever meant.*
*It is the same as it ever was.*
*There is absolute unbroken continuity.*
*What is death but a negligible accident?*
*Why should I be out of mind*
*Because I am out of sight?*
*I am waiting for you for an interval.*
*Somewhere very near,*
*Just around the corner.*
*All is well.*
*Nothing is past; nothing is lost.*
*One brief moment and all will be as it was before.*
*How we shall laugh at the trouble of parting when we meet again!*

~ Canon Henry Scott-Holland

Stages of bereavement and some of the emotions already discussed in the previous section, will now be looked at in more detail. The experience of past events and coming to terms with your loss can trigger a variety of emotions. Reasons why you may be experiencing these will be explored, along with suggestions on how to move away from these often-limiting beliefs. Be reassured, that you are not alone, many of the past events listed below are commonly felt by caregivers going through a dementia related bereavement.

# Past Events Triggering Guilt

Some possible reasons for feeling guilty

- Did you spend time during the illness, despondent about how your relationship had changed with your loved one? Maybe you dwelled on the thoughts of 'why is this happening to me'?

- Did you struggle to look after your loved one in their own home? Do you still feel guilty that carers, respite care or long-term care in a residential or nursing home was needed?

- Did you at times wish that your loved one's dementia would end while they were living, but now feel guilty about feeling this way when you would do anything to see them just one more time?

- Are you now experiencing guilt as you recall how frustrated and angry you became at times with your loved one?

Ways that may help you to move on from this emotion:

- Recognise that your response to your loved one having dementia is normal; many relationships are deeply affected by this illness.

- Not everyone is a 'natural born' carer and looking after your loved one 24/7 with such a complex illness is difficult.
- Watching a loved one endure dementia is difficult. It is understandable that you would want them to be released from this life destroying illness.
- Any negative reaction to this illness is not unusual. Most caregivers in a similar situation will tell you that they also experienced times when they became frustrated and angry too. None of us are 'superhuman'.

## My own thoughts about the 'guilt' I still experience...

## Steps I can take to move myself away from these feelings of guilt…

# Past Events Causing Anxiety

Some possible reasons for feeling anxious:

- Are you experiencing ongoing anxieties related to financial struggles or dealing with legal matters?
- Do you suffer from 'flashbacks' related to the unpleasant memories caused by your loved one's illness?
- Are you still having difficulty moving on with your own life?
- Are you struggling to come to terms with the fact that you are not able to see your loved one again?

Ways that may help you to move on from this emotion:

- Seek advice from your solicitor, bank or financial advisor.
- Talk to those closest to you or consider having some counselling. Don't bottle up your emotions.
- Be kind to yourself and try to relax by listening to calming music or start meditation or deep breathing exercises. Plan things, however small, that you can look forward to.

- Even though your loved one is at peace, it will still take some adjusting to life without them. Give yourself time to heal.

## My own thoughts about the 'anxiety' I still experience...

## Steps I can take to move myself away from feeling anxious…

# Past Events Causing Anger

Some possible reasons for feeling angry:

- Are you still feeling angry about the illness and how it affected you and your loved one?
- Do you feel angry with the limited support received by professionals, family and friends?
- Do you feel angry that there is still no cure or effective treatment for dementia?
- If poor standards of care were received from a hospital or care home setting, has this triggered an ongoing angry reaction in you?

Ways that may help you to move on from this emotion:

- No one can prepare themselves for the effects that an illness like dementia will have on them. Recognise that at times we need to rationalise what has gone on in the past, however dwelling on such thoughts will not be beneficial to you in the long term.

- Instead of focusing on the limited support received from others, try to be proud of the support that you gave to your loved one.

- It may help you to feel like you are making a difference by fundraising for one of the dementia charities that will invest money into valuable research.

- Put forward a complaint or concern with the professional body responsible for your loved one's care, if you feel this will benefit you in moving forward with a problem you had about their care when they were living. You may not be able to change what happened to your loved one, however it may prevent someone else going through a similar experience.

## My own thoughts about the anger I still experience...

______________________________

______________________________

______________________________

______________________________

______________________________

______________________________

______________________________

## Steps I can take to move myself away from feeling angry…

# Past Events Causing Envy

Some possible reasons for feeling envy:

- As a caregiver, you may have often said to yourself, 'why me'? Especially when other people you know were still 'living' their own life.
- Your long-term dreams and goals for the future may have been destroyed after your loved one's diagnosis. You may have become envious watching other people you know fulfilling similar dreams to you.
- Did you feel envious of others that had a better financial situation than you because their loved one still worked?
- Do you feel that your life is 'standing still' while you struggle to come to terms with your own bereavement? Perhaps you are envious of other members of your family who now appear to be moving on with their own life.

Ways that may help you to move on from this emotion:

- Off-load your feelings to someone you trust who will not

judge you or alternatively you may choose to write your feelings down. Reassess where you are with your own life now.

- Try as much as possible to put envious feelings from the past aside and move on by concentrating on the life you now have ahead of you. What things can you do now that will make you happy?
- Avoid comparing your financial situation to those around you, it will only make you feel worse. Instead seek financial advice to ensure you are in the best position you can be with your cashflow.
- It may be difficult but take steps to make plans for your future; begin by doing a small thing each week that you enjoy.

## My own thoughts about the envy I still experience...

______________________________________________

______________________________________________

______________________________________________

______________________________________________

______________________________________________

______________________________________________

Steps I can take to move myself away from feeling envy…

# Past Events Causing Loneliness and Isolation

Some possible reasons for still feeling lonely and isolated:

- Are you feeling lonely and isolated, since losing your loved one? Perhaps you are finding it difficult to go out and socialise.
- Do you miss the residents, visitors and staff from the care home where your loved one once lived? This may be especially so if they were there for many years and you visited on a regular basis.
- Have you lost contact with family and friends since your loved one's illness progressed?
- Were you involved in dementia support groups that you may feel you should no longer attend since your loved one has died?

Ways that may help you to move on from this emotion:

- Try to occupy yourself as much as possible. You may want

to try a new hobby or pastime or offer to look after younger members of your family or their pets while your loved ones are at work.

- If it feels appropriate, you may want to keep in touch with the staff or families connected to the care home. If it is not too painful you may decide to continue to visit the home or offer to do some voluntary work.
- Attempt to re-kindle friendships with people you have not seen in a long time. Social media can be a good way of getting in touch or alternatively you may decide to write them a letter or give them a telephone call.
- It might take a lot of courage but try to join new groups that interest you locally. You may also want to consider setting up a group with other caregivers that have also lost loved ones to dementia.

## My own thoughts about the loneliness and isolation I still experience...

Steps I can take to move myself away from feeling lonely and isolated…

# Past Events Causing Regret

Some reasons why you may be feeling regretful:

- Do you still regret making the decision to put them into long term care? Maybe you felt that you chose the wrong care home?

- Did you struggle to 'accept' your loved one's illness? Maybe you avoided going to see them because you found their dementia difficult to cope with?

- Are you regretful for the things you were not able to achieve together? Like the enjoyment of retirement or not being able to share special occasions such as anniversaries or weddings.

- Do you feel regret for the times that you shouted at your loved one for not doing something right even though you knew it was the illness and not them personally?

Ways that may help you to move on from feeling regretful:

- Acknowledge that you cared for them as well as you could,

given the situation you were in. If the care they received was not good this was the failings of the care home and not you.

- Don't focus too much on your reaction to your loved one's dementia. Recognise that your continued love made watching them endure dementia more difficult for you.

- Try to reflect on the positive memories you still have of special times that you both shared, rather than dwelling on the things that they will no longer be able to be part of.

- Always remember that you weren't purposely shouting at your loved one, it was their 'illness' and not them that made you feel this way.

## My own thoughts about the regret that I still experience...

## Steps I can take to move myself away from feeling regretful…

*'Losing people you love affects you. It is buried inside of you and becomes this big, deep hole of ache. It doesn't magically go away, even when you stop officially mourning.'*

*~ Carrie Jones*

**Here is space to write any other emotions which you are currently experiencing.**

## Past Events Causing ____________________

Some reasons why you may be feeling ____________________

- 
- 
- 
- 

Ways that may help you to move on from feeling ______________

- 
- 
- 
- 

## My own thoughts about the ____________ that I still experience

________________________________________

________________________________________

________________________________________

________________________________________

________________________________________

________________________________________

________________________________________

________________________________________

________________________________________

________________________________________

________________________________________

________________________________________

________________________________________

## Steps I can take to move myself away from feeling ____________________

______________________________________________

______________________________________________

______________________________________________

______________________________________________

______________________________________________

______________________________________________

______________________________________________

______________________________________________

______________________________________________

______________________________________________

## Past Events Causing ____________________

Some reasons why you may be feeling ____________________

- 
- 
- 
- 

Ways that may help you to move on from feeling _________

- 
- 
- 
- 

## My own thoughts about the ___________ that I experience

____________________________________________

____________________________________________

____________________________________________

____________________________________________

____________________________________________

____________________________________________

____________________________________________

____________________________________________

____________________________________________

____________________________________________

____________________________________________

____________________________________________

# Steps I can take to move myself away from feeling

____________________

## Final Thoughts

My final words as we come to the end of this section, is to encourage you to take positive actions and thoughts, however small, to move yourself away from any negative emotions associated with your loved one's dementia illness and subsequent bereavement.

Difficult as I know it will be, try not to focus too much on the bad times you both went through. Always remember that it was the illness and not your loved one. Don't feel guilty if you now find yourself feeling relieved that your journey with dementia has now ended. This is a normal human reaction to the 'loss' of the illness and not to the 'loss' of your loved one. Be reconciled with thoughts that they are no longer suffering and are now at peace.

As you move on with your own life, I am certain that your loved one would wish for you to get back to some form of 'normality' in the best way you can. With this in mind, we will now plan the next chapter of your life and look at the last two sections of this book, to find new ways of helping you cope with your ongoing journey.

# Further Thoughts

# SECTION 4

## Helping You Cope

### She Is Gone (He Is Gone)

*You can shed tears that she is gone,*
*Or you can smile because she has lived.*
*You can close your eyes and pray that she will come back,*
*Or you can open your eyes and see all that she has left.*
*Your heart can be empty because you can't see her,*
*Or you can be full of the love that you shared.*

*You can turn your back on tomorrow*
*and live yesterday,*
*Or you can be happy for tomorrow*
*because of yesterday.*
*You can remember her and only that*
*she is gone,*
*Or you can cherish her memory and let*
*it live on.*
*You can cry and close your mind, be*
*empty and turn your back,*
*Or you can do what she would want:*
*smile, open your eyes, love and go on.*

~ *David Harkins*

Section four will focus on a variety of coping strategies you may like to try to help you live day-to-day with your bereavement. Grief, as discussed previously, is an individual process, so not everything mentioned in this section will feel comfortable or even appropriate to you. I urge you to try the coping strategies that interest you, while ignoring the ones that fail to move you forward.

# Looking For Signs

Some people believe that when their loved one has passed over they leave them signs to show that they are still around. A classic example of this is discovering a white feather which appears to arrive from nowhere. I have personally found a few of these, with very little explanation on how they got there at the time!

'Signs' will vary from person to person, as they will often relate to something that is significant to you or to the person who has passed over. For example, I associate the sound made by pigeons with my grandad because when he was alive, he kept racing pigeons. In a similar way, I think about my grandmother when I see robins as she used to love feeding the robin that visited her garden.

No one can ever be certain that these 'signs' are a true indication that our loved ones are around us, however I personally experience more 'signs' during the times when I need more comfort and support. Whether this is reality or not, I can never be certain. However, it still gives me reassurance to think they could still be close by when I need them most.

Another experience with signs that had an impact on my life several years ago, was when I was visiting my friend's grave. My friend was young when she passed away from cancer. She is buried in a beautiful woodland cemetery in the countryside, a distance from where I live. One day I decided to go and visit her grave, which I hadn't been to since her funeral several years before. My friend was one of the first to be buried there, so I was shocked to find that there was now a lot more graves. I searched but struggled to find where she was and was about to give up, feeling very disappointed when I noticed two bees, dancing around a gravestone near to where I was standing. I have always had a phobia of bees and wasps since I was a young child, so they were the 'perfect' thing to capture my attention! To my amazement, they were flying around my friend's grave and without them I would never have found it. I sat down on a nearby bench and watched the bees until they flew off. After spending some time deep in thought about the many happy times we shared, I got up and walked to my car. As I opened my car door another bee flew straight pass my face making me stand back quickly. Even to this day, I'd like to think that these bees were a sign from my friend helping me find where she was and possibly even saying goodbye as I was leaving, too.

These are just a few of my own experiences that relate to 'signs'. You may have experienced similar ones or in the future discover new signs that resonate with you. See them as a sign of comfort, as well as a lovely way to keep the memory of your loved one alive.

## My thoughts on looking for signs…

## Signs that I have experienced…

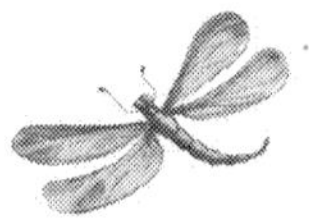

# Comforting Things

It may be a great source of comfort to have some personal things that you can cherish as a reminder of your loved one. This may be an item of clothing, a piece of jewellery or an ornament that they once loved.

My own personal example of this is a wedding ring left to me by my step grandmother that I always wear and in my dining room I also have two small poppy vases that belonged to my great grandmother.

Perhaps you can treasure an item that your loved one made, like a piece of furniture, a tapestry or a painting. Such items may help you to connect with your memories when you need to be close to them.

You may like to also create a memorial garden, that can be used as an area of reminiscence. You could grow their favourite plants and flowers, have a memorial plaque made with some meaningful words or purchase a water feature or similar garden ornament.

There are also companies that can make jewellery, photo frames and glass sculptures from your loved one's ashes. For some people this may be a great source of comfort and something to cherish. Such companies can be found on the internet, however, do some research into their products first by looking at their reviews and feedback before ordering.

Having an item that brings you closer to your loved one does not need to be complicated, something as simple as a small photograph of them carried around in a locket, purse, wallet or mobile phone case may be all you need to feel reassured that they are always with you.

## My thoughts on comforting things...

# Items that could be a source of comfort to me...

# PAULA'S MEMORY BEARS

I came across Paula's Memory Bears on Facebook and thought what a lovely idea this was to remember and treasure something personal from your loved one. Paula makes bears, animals and cushions from a cherished piece of clothing which was once worn by them. Everything she creates is unique, as the pictures of her finished products illustrate.

Below is Paula's story on how she started her business. The links to her Facebook and website pages are also included.

'I found a wonderful way in honouring a loved one by making bears and animals for ones that have lost someone so dear to them. I decided to do this because I lost my daddy Allan. I started 'Memory Bears from the Heart' by Paula in memory of him. I have been a seamstress for over 20 years and decided to make memories also. I started by making my family bears first and went from there. It was so hard at first, but I knew all these bears would help my wonderful family. I wanted to give people and children something to cherish to help with the loss of a loved one. Each bear is a wonderful keepsake. These bears are as unique as the person/persons they represent.'

*'I once was worn by someone so dear,*

*Who through loving memory will always be here.'*

Memory Bears From The Heart By Paula/Sewing Alterations

www.memorybearsfromtheheartbypaula.co.uk

# Memory Box or Book

Always try to reflect on the good memories spent with your loved one, by creating a photo album or scrapbook based on your loved one's life. You could use photographs taken from their childhood, places that they loved to visit or stories that you can recall from family gatherings and celebrations. Other memorabilia like tickets from a concert, leaflets from days out or postcards from their holidays could also be included. Write as much information as you can, so that future generations of your family have an understanding of your loved one in years to come.

If you would like an alternative to a photo album or scrapbook, you may like to create a memory box full of items that remind you or used to belong to your loved one. This could include small ornaments that they once treasured, pressed flowers from their funeral wreath or birthday cards they wrote for you when they were well.

Here are some more suggestions you may like to use:

- Personal items like their glasses or their hairbrush
- An item of jewellery or their watch
- Personal memorabilia like medals, trophies and

certificates

- A lock of their hair
- Their favourite perfume or aftershave
- Information about their life, for example
    - where they grew up
    - where they worked
    - their favourite food and drink
    - their favourite colour
    - favourite flower
    - where they liked to visit or go on holiday
    - their pastimes and hobbies
    - a small family tree or a brief history on their siblings, cousins etc
    - things they achieved or were proud of
    - family pets
    - favourite poem, song or hymn
- The order of service from their funeral
- Their favourite book
- A small item of clothing

Creating a memory box or book dedicated to your loved one can be both a rewarding and therapeutic process. It also provides you with something to cherish and a means of keeping their memory alive, when reminiscing about them.

## My thoughts on creating a memory box or book...

# Items I could use…

# Surrounding Yourself With Meaningful Music

Music has a magical way of changing a person's mood depending on the type of music being played and the memories that it triggers. For instance, music that is upbeat and lively may make you feel happy and energetic, hearing a love song may put you in a romantic mood and soothing music may help you to relax or fall asleep.

Hearing a certain song or a piece of music, may help to trigger memories related to an event that has happened in your life. For example, you may have chosen some music to be played at your wedding, which when you hear it now instantly gives you a memory of that day. In a similar way, a certain type of music or a song being played may remind you of your loved one. Music related to them may initially be too 'raw' to hear, however as time progresses it may become a great source of comfort to you.

Hearing a piece of music that has meaning to you, may not always be solely related to the tune being played; the lyrics of a song may also resonate with you too. Through the years there has been many songs written about loss. Listen carefully to the words as they may help you at a time when you need them most.

Examples of songs related to loss:

**Eric Clapton: 'Tears in Heaven'**

Would I know your name

If I saw you in heaven?

Would it be the same

If I saw you in heaven

I must be strong and carry on

'Cause I know I don't belong here in heaven.

**The Beatles: 'Let It Be'**

And when the broken-hearted people living in the world agree

There will be an answer, let it be

For though they may be parted, there is still a chance that they will see

There will be an answer, let it be.

## Queen: 'The Show Must Go On'

The show must go on

The show must go on, yeah

Inside my heart is breaking

My make-up may be flaking

But my smile still stays on.

## My thoughts on meaningful music…

## Music that brings comfort to me…

## Music that helps to improve my mood…

List the songs that help to improve your mood. Play them as often as you can, especially during times when you are struggling to feel happy.

## My Top Ten Playlist

1)

2)

3)

4)

5)

6)

7)

8)

9)

10)

# Bereavement Support

While your loved one was still living you may have attended your local dementia support group or been part of a dementia group on a social media site like Facebook. Since they have passed away the type of support you are now looking for may appear to be quite limited. I am not sure if there are any bereavement support groups following a dementia illness in the areas where you live; it does appear that if there are any, they are generally few and far between. It would be especially beneficial if the support group is related to losing someone to dementia, if not then you may want to consider setting one up yourself. This doesn't need to be complex and can involve a small group of you meeting up on a regular basis at a local café. Try to keep a balance of offloading the bad times or the more challenging aspects of your bereavement with a reflection on the good times and happy memories too.

One of the main reasons why I decided to write this book was because I felt that many families are often left to face this part of their journey alone. Support can be limited at a time when it is crucial that the right type of help is offered, especially if you are still trying to make sense of negative feelings and unhappy memories associated with this type of 'double' bereavement. Just because your loved one is no longer here, doesn't mean that your own personal journey with 'their dementia illness' has ended. I am sure many of you would say that your journey with dementia never ends, due to the huge impact it has had on your life. Give yourself time to come to terms with your loss, however, seek professional help, as mentioned previously, if you are still struggling.

## My thoughts on bereavement support…

# Sharing Your Experience

My dementia business 'Make Way For Tomorrow' involves supporting caregivers, both during and after losing their loved ones to dementia. Every story I listen to is unique, as no two people exposed to this type of illness will go on to identically share the same experiences. Expressing what has gone on in your journey during these times can help you come to terms with the impact that dementia has had on you. You may have already spoken about or written down your experiences of what you went through when your loved one was still living, like Dawn did with her mother's dementia. Your onward journey may now also benefit from doing something similar.

Any written thoughts are personal to you and do not need to be shared. The process of writing your thoughts down onto a piece of paper or in a notebook can be a therapeutic tool in moving forward with your bereavement.

You may already be aware that some caregivers have written books about their own journey with dementia to help others in a similar situation. Knowing that your own story with dementia may in the future help someone else, could provide you with some much-needed comfort, as you move forward with your life.

For some, writing down your own experiences may not resonate with you, however you may take comfort instead by reading other people's experiences, as you discover you were not alone with some of the things that you went through.

Well known people, like former news reader John Suchet, wrote a book called 'My Bonnie: How dementia stole the love of my life' which tells the story of the progression of his wife Bonnie's dementia and similarly, Fiona Phillips remembered for her early morning breakfast programme, wrote 'Before I Forget' based on her experiences of having both parents affected by dementia. There are also many books written by non-famous people who still have a passion to get their story across. One such lady is Jane Moore who has written a book about her mum called: 'Dementia and Nellie Dean' (Available as a Kindle download on Amazon).

Jane had this to say about her book...

'Nellie Dean was known to many on a Facebook page called Dementia Aware as my mother who had Alzheimer's and Vascular Dementia. Later my mother was to help me start a Purple Angel dementia-inclusive community in our town. Through education and understanding we lived 'better'. The disease was devasting for Mum but also for our whole family. Many people write their stories leaving a message for the future. I simply want everyone to know how brave my mother was and mention some of the things that I learnt on the way.'

# My thoughts on sharing my experience…

# Being Around People

Spending time with those closest to you, can be a great form of support and comfort. Whether they are your family, friends or neighbours, being able to share happy memories or just offloading what's on your mind, can be quite therapeutic. Try to meet up regularly with people who you can easily talk to or those that instantly cheer you up and make you laugh.

It's understandable that you may not feel like going out and socialising initially after losing your loved one. Give yourself time to come to terms with your loss. When you start to feel comfortable, take small steps and return to some form of 'normality' by meeting up with people you feel relaxed with. This could simply involve going out for a quiet meal or a visit to the cinema.

There may be days when you only want to be in the company of those who once knew your loved one, so that memories of times spent together can be shared. However, there could be other occasions, when you want to distract yourself from your bereavement, and prefer to be with people who didn't know your loved one, like a work colleague.

In time, you may want to start socialising more and may consider joining a group activity like a dance class, amateur football team or local church group. Or alternatively you could take up a new course or hobby, where you can meet new people and keep socially active.

## My thoughts on being around people…

# How To Cope With Memorable Days

Memorable days will always be difficult, when they are related to the person you have lost. They can be emotionally challenging especially in the first year of your loved one's death. For example, the first time you have a wedding anniversary without them being there to celebrate it with you or the day of your loved one's birthday when you are unable to buy them their usual birthday card and presents.

Christmas is often a challenging time too, especially in the first few years of a bereavement. It is often portrayed as a fun-filled day spent with family, however for some, it can be a very painful and emotional time too. Try to surround yourself with your loved ones and support each other during this difficult time. Having young children in the family may help, as you will probably have more of a reason to ensure the day is special for them. You may want to consider a change to the 'normal' Christmas rituals, by doing something completely different, like going out for dinner or going away for a few days.

It is inevitable that the anniversary of your loved one's death will conjure up many painful memories related to their final days, hours and minutes. During this time, you may find yourself reflecting more on the events both leading up to and after their death. There is often no easy way to get through this day. Being distracted by work or keeping busy may help, or alternatively, you may benefit by spending time quietly on your own or visiting their grave or the place where their ashes were scattered.

The first year of 'memorable' days without your loved one can often be the most challenging. Praise yourself for getting through these difficult days and don't be too hard on yourself if you find you are struggling with your emotions during this time. It may feel appropriate and a source of comfort, to do something special in memory of your loved one. For example:

- lighting a candle
- take some flowers to their resting place
- write a death or birthday memorial to put in your local paper
- have a meal in their honour
- go to a memorable place that they once loved to visit
- spend some time in nature, remembering the special times you shared

# Things to do on memorable days...

Special things I would like to do on their birthday

1) ______________________________

2) ______________________________

3) ______________________________

Special things I would like to do on the memorial of their death

1) ______________________________

2) ______________________________

3) ______________________________

Special things I would like to do on an anniversary or memorable event

1) ______________________________

2) ______________________________

3) ______________________________

# My thoughts on memorable days...

# Fundraising and Memory Walks

It may help you in your bereavement process, to consider doing something for a dementia-related charity. Being able to help others affected by the illness, as well as the satisfaction of raising money and awareness for such a good cause, can be of benefit for all concerned. A lady I know did a sponsored walk up Ben Nevis, dedicated to the memory of her husband shortly after he died. She spoke afterwards about this being good therapy, as she was raising awareness and money for her chosen dementia charity, as well as keeping her husband's memory alive.

There are many ways to raise money. You may decide to do a sponsored walk or run, a bungee jump (for the brave!) or arrange a coffee morning or table-top sale.

The charity you choose may be a local organisation that have helped you during your dementia journey, a national dementia charity raising money for some much-needed research or even the 'residents' comfort fund' in the care home where your loved one was looked after.

'Memory walks' are another way to remember your loved one and all those who have passed away or still living with dementia. Walks of this nature are normally listed on dementia charity websites or advertised locally. They often take place around 'Dementia Action Weeks' or 'Dementia Awareness Days'. I've personally taken part in quite a few. There is always a lovely atmosphere, as well as a sense of pride on doing something to keep your loved one's memory alive. It is an opportunity to meet other people who have also had their lives affected by dementia too.

## My thoughts on fundraising and memory walks...

# Further Thoughts

# SECTION 5

## The Future

### Let Me Go

*When I come to the end of the road*
*And the sun has set for me*
*I want no rites in a gloom filled room*
*Why cry for a soul set free?*
*Miss me a little, but not for long*
*And not with your head bowed low.*
*Remember the love that once we shared*
*Miss me, but let me go.*
*For this is a journey we all must take*
*And each must go alone.*
*It's all part of the master plan*

*A step on the road to home.*
*When you are lonely and sick at heart*
*Go to the friends we know.*
*Laugh at all the things we used to do*
*Miss me, but let me go.*
*When I am dead, my dearest*
*Sing no sad songs for me.*
*Plant thou no roses at my head*
*Nor shady cypress tree.*
*Be the green grass above me*
*With showers and dewdrops wet.*
*And if thou wilt, remember*
*And if thou wilt, forget.*
*I shall not see the shadows,*
*I shall not fear the rain;*
*I shall not hear the nightingale*
*Sing on as if in pain;*
*And dreaming through the twilight*
*That doth not rise nor set,*
*Haply I may remember,*
*And haply may forget.*

~ Christina Rosetti

In this final section, we will incorporate some of the areas already discussed and discover how you can now look ahead, with your future wellbeing at the forefront of your mind. This could depend on you finding ways to cope on a daily basis or just by trying to live in the moment. It is inevitable that you may still experience a mixture of good and bad days. Something as simple as a passing memory or a song played on the radio, may trigger an unexpected emotional reaction. You may never fully lose those feelings associated with grief, as loved ones will always be missed. However, it is hoped that the impact of such feelings over time, will become much easier to live with.

# Reflecting On The Good Times

Spend time reflecting on the good times and memories that you and your loved one shared. This is essential because the impact of their dementia illness can leave you with a lot of negative thoughts. 'Living' the dementia journey with your loved one will have had a huge effect on you and the rest of your family too. If your loved one was still living, they would not want you to dwell on negative memories that their dementia illness created. Instead they would only want you to fondly remember the good times that you both shared.

It is inevitable that the more challenging events associated with the illness may start to creep into your mind from time to time. When this happens quickly replace them with a happier time that you both spent together. For example, you may find yourself dwelling on the weight loss your loved one suffered towards the end of their illness and how they would often refuse to eat. Change this type of thought with a happier memory, perhaps associated with your loved one's favourite restaurant and the meals you have all enjoyed eating there.

Altering such thoughts may appear like a challenging process at first, however I do urge you to persevere with it, because it will start to become easier the more often you do it.

Make a list of some of the happy memories that you and your loved one shared together. You may find it useful to revisit this list as a distraction, from any negative thoughts that start to come into your mind.

1) ________________________________

________________________________

________________________________

________________________________

________________________________

2) ________________________________

________________________________

________________________________

________________________________

________________________________

3) ________________________________

________________________________

________________________________

________________________________

________________________________

4) ______________________________

______________________________

______________________________

______________________________

______________________________

5) ______________________________

______________________________

______________________________

______________________________

______________________________

## My thoughts associated with 'reflecting on the good times'…

______________________________

______________________________

______________________________

______________________________

______________________________

______________________________

______________________________

______________________________

______________________________

# Ways To Let Go, While Finding Peace Within Yourself

Time spent dwelling on the challenging times that the illness caused is a common theme throughout this book because it is often thought by many as one of the major obstacles to overcome when losing a loved one to dementia. Achieving some form of peace within yourself can be difficult, as it will often rely upon you being able to come to terms with their dementia and the impact it's had on you.

You may still be holding on to negative emotions like guilt, resentment or frustration. If this is the case, sections two and three will help you to acknowledge the reason why you are feeling like this. We can never change previous events even though there are instances where we would love to do so. Perhaps in the past you have acted on impulse and shouted at your loved one or they may have unintentionally hurt you. The key thing to always remember is that it was not you or them that was at fault, it was the 'illness'.

None of us can predict how we would react when presented with an illness like dementia. We are all unique individuals and so it is only human nature for us to react differently to any given situation or circumstance.

If you find yourself still struggling to let go, doing the forgiveness process below may help.

## The Forgiveness Process

Write down all the negative things associated with your dementia journey, that you are still holding on to since your loved one has died. You may want to forgive the dementia illness, a certain situation, yourself (if you felt you didn't handle something appropriately) or the way another member of your family behaved.

Once you have done this, look at your list and difficult as it may be, forgive everything that is on it. (Remember that forgiveness doesn't mean what went on was right, it is just an acknowledgement to say it will no longer have such a detrimental effect on your life).

Inform your 'inner self' that it is now time to move on from these thoughts, as they are holding you back and having a significant impact on your future happiness.

When you feel you have fully released all your negative thoughts, emotions and experiences, destroy the paper by shredding, ripping it up or, if safe to do so, burn it.

You may need to repeat this process until you have achieved complete forgiveness. The 'forgiveness process' can be repeated in the future with any new challenges that you face.

You may have found during your dementia journey, that emotions were often running high from either yourself or other members of your family that caused conflicts between you. Perhaps you have been left with a situation where not all of you have moved on from this, and grudges may still be held. It is important to recognise that both yourself and others were going through a heightened emotional rollercoaster and maybe now is the time to make peace from the events of the past. Whatever your own situation is, endeavour to move away from wishing that you or others could have behaved better or that circumstances should have been different.

Often our biggest critic in life is our self, vented through our own inner voice. Negative 'self-talk' about past events, will be of no benefit at all. We can never change what has happened previously. Instead, we can 'grow and learn' from these events, while making peace with ourselves along the way.

Another way to help you gain peace from past events is illustrated in the table below. It gives an example of a past event that you may still feel uneasy about, along with a rationale to help you move forward. There is space for you to write any of your own situations that you presently find yourself in.

| Situation from a past event that I still feel uneasy about | Rationalising what went on in order to feel peace with this situation |
|---|---|
| Putting my loved one in a care home because I was no longer able to take care of them | For their wellbeing and safety, they needed this 24-hour care |
| | |
| | |
| | |
| | |

# My thoughts on finding ways of 'letting go and making peace with myself'...

# Learning From Your Bereavement Process

We all grieve at a different pace and bereavement will affect us in various ways. Perhaps you have experienced times when you thought you were coming to terms with your loss, only to suddenly hit a low point, that sends you many steps back. Situations like this, may have happened to you several times already and can be difficult to move on from. You may especially be concerned that such times could reoccur in the future too and wonder how you will cope if this happens again.

Don't be too despondent and feel that you are not moving on from your bereavement when your emotions run high. It is essential to avoid 'bottling things up' which could over a period of time, cause a more detrimental effect on your well-being.

When experiencing these 'low points' try writing your feelings down or if you prefer, talk to someone you know will listen in a non-judgemental way. Sharing your thoughts will help you to understand your own emotional triggers, for instance, the situations or events that make you feel better or worse.

Here are some examples of reflective questions, that you could use to either talk or write about:

What has made me feel sad today?

It's been several months since my loved one's death, why do I not feel any better?

Why do certain circumstances trigger an emotional reaction in me?

Would I have experienced such intense grief, if my loved one hadn't had dementia?

__________________________________________________________

__________________________________________________________

__________________________________________________________

__________________________________________________________

__________________________________________________________

I feel guilty that I now want to move on and enjoy the rest of my life I have left. Is it right to feel like this?

__________________________________________________________

__________________________________________________________

__________________________________________________________

__________________________________________________________

__________________________________________________________

If the above reflective questions do not reside with you and your own personal bereavement, think about the sort of questions that will help you to explore your own thoughts and feelings. The type of questions you ask yourself will probably vary from time to time, depending on what you are experiencing and events that are happening in your life.

Writing your thoughts down regularly will help you to keep a check on your own personal grief and you may be surprised when reading back through it how far you have actually progressed. Starting out, you may initially want to reflect on how you are feeling on a daily basis, however in time, this may change to weekly or when something significant happens in your life.

## Thoughts I have on 'learning about myself from my bereavement process'…

___________________________________________

___________________________________________

___________________________________________

___________________________________________

___________________________________________

___________________________________________

___________________________________________

___________________________________________

___________________________________________

___________________________________________

___________________________________________

# Give Yourself Time

It is commonly said that 'time' is a great healer. However, not everyone goes on to experience this concept. You may be personally still struggling and find it difficult to comprehend the full impact that your loved one's dementia has had on you, both during and after their illness. Perhaps you also feel that you are frequently re-living your 'loss' when faced with memorable days, vivid dreams or recalling distressing memories related to your loved one. Don't be too hard on yourself if you just feel like crying out loud or venting your frustrations.

In your own time, you will start to go forward with your life again. It will help if you have things to look forward to, as well as surrounding yourself with people you can trust and that are supportive, like close family and friends.

There may be moments when you feel you have forgotten how to be happy. If this happens, reflect on the things in the past that have taken you to a happier place and revisit these events, if possible, again. Even taking just small steps to creating a 'happier' you is a positive direction to go in.

List 5 things that make you happy:

1)

2)

3)

4)

5)

## Steps you can take to achieve these things...

## Any final thoughts you may have about 'giving yourself time'...

# Acts of Kindness

Struggling with being able to lift your mood will be having an impact, as well as preventing you from moving on with your life the best way you can. We have already discussed things that you can do to make yourself feel happier, however, you may want to consider doing small acts of kindness too. They can potentially act as mood enhancers, as well as provide you with the knowledge that you are doing something worthwhile, for the benefit of others. Acts of kindness don't need to be complicated and can involve a variety of things. For example, fundraising for your favourite charity or doing some voluntary work to help your local community.

Here are some more examples you may like to try...

1) Give a compliment to someone you know

2) Buy a drink or a snack for a homeless person

3) Take an elderly relative to a hospital appointment

4) Gift a lottery ticket to a friend

5) Donate unused presents to charity

6) Take the bins out for your neighbour

7) Send a friend a thank you card as an appreciation of their support

8) Be gracious on the road and allow traffic to come through, even if it is your right of way

9) Cook a meal for a relative or friend

10) Buy a small gift for someone special and surprise them with it

Acts of kindness I may like to try…

1) ____________________________________________

____________________________________________

2) ____________________________________________

____________________________________________

3) ____________________________________________

____________________________________________

4) ____________________________________________

____________________________________________

5) ____________________________________________

____________________________________________

## Any further thoughts I may have on doing 'acts of kindness'...

# Mood Boosters

It is inevitable that your mood will be low, as you adjust to life without your loved one. However, it is important for your future wellbeing to aim for a balance of emotions, by slowly introducing those things into your life that bring you happiness. Endeavour to do things you enjoy as regularly as possible. As time progresses, try to focus on increasing the length and the number of things that create 'happy times' for you. This will help to guide your life in a more positive direction.

Trying to enhance your mood, can be achieved through doing simple things like eating your favourite foods, going to the cinema, gardening, baking, fishing or having your hair done. Schedule as many 'mood boosters' into your week as possible, with an aim each day to do something that makes you happy, however small this may be.

A typical week could look like this:

Monday - Swimming

Tuesday - Cinema

Wednesday - Baking

Thursday - Hair done

Friday - Cook my favourite meal

Saturday - Fun day with my children or grandchildren

Sunday - Spending time walking in nature or gardening

Spend time reflecting on the things that make you happy, as this can also help to promote a positive mood. This could involve you reminiscing about your favourite place, memories of your grandchildren playing or just recalling how you feel when you sunbathe in the warm sunshine. Picture these happy thoughts and memories somewhere comfortable and quiet and if possible, with your eyes closed. Enhance the images in your mind by making them appear brighter, while bringing your attention to any sounds and smells related to the pictures in your mind. Throughout this process, concentrate on feeling relaxed and regulate your breathing by slowing down your inhale and exhale breaths.

Feeling good about your appearance will also help to lift your mood. We all know how we feel when we have a 'bad hair day'! This can often make us feel inwardly unhappy and affects our confidence. Wearing clothes that are dark and drab could also have a prolonged effect on our mood. Try wearing more bright and colourful clothing or add a colourful accessory like a scarf or an item of jewellery to an outfit. Spending a bit of time on the way you look whether it's through styling your hair, having a shave or putting on your favourite perfume or aftershave can help you to feel more positive about yourself.

Endeavour to smile as often as possible because even though at times you may not feel like it, it can stimulate our brain and make us 'feel good'. Smiling and laughter can also help to reduce stress, release emotions, expand your lungs, exercise your body, provide a natural pain relief and positively attract people to you.

When the time feels right, you may want to consider doing a big spring clean around your home or attempt some home improvements. Decluttering by getting rid of the things you no longer need or revamping a room may help you to feel happier in your environment and provide you with something to focus on.

Playing a particular piece of music can quickly change our mood. For example, sad songs can often make us feel emotional, whereas 'upbeat' and cheerful songs can help to pull us out of a despondent state of mind. More thoughts on this can be found in Section 4.

Other things that I could do to improve my mood...

1) ______________________________

2) ______________________________

3) ______________________________

4) ______________________________

5) ______________________________

6) ______________________________

7) ______________________________

8) ______________________________

9) ______________________________

10) ______________________________

## Any further thoughts on 'mood boosters'...

# GRATITUDE FOR THE SMALL THINGS

Having a sense of gratitude for the small things in life could be just one way of helping you to cope on a daily basis. Some days, as you have probably already discovered, are easier to survive than others. When the more challenging moments arrive, try to think of just one positive thing that has also occurred to make you feel grateful, this could be as simple as enjoying a lovely milky drink before you go to bed or a long soak in the bath. Continue to acknowledge that every day has a silver lining, even though it may not always feel like this at the time.

Ali Gill is an author who has written a wonderful book called 'My Perfect Journal'. The concept behind the book was to help the reader find a 'perfect' in every day, which was inspired by events that had gone on in Ali's own life, as she describes below.

## Hidden Perfects

Having been visited by the 'black dog' on more occasions than I would like to admit, I ended up at a point where I crashed both mentally and physically. I was not being a good mum, good wife or a good friend (or so I thought) and I most certainly didn't like myself very much at all. When I hit my brick wall I totally crumbled and realised I had to do something. I started to look for one good thing in each day and logged them, even the smallest of things at times would get into my journal! A nice sound, a kind word, a cuppa, the sunshine. Glimmers of hope and of positivity that made the days bearable, if not sometimes slightly more enjoyable. Slowly my journey led me to creating a gratitude journal to help others in similar situations or even those in a great place that just wanted somewhere to log the good stuff! My Perfect Journal was a long and painful process in creating due to my own limiting beliefs. The journal was eventually launched at the end of 2017 to brilliant feedback and lovely reviews and people saying how much it was helping them. It is a journal that is undated, full of inspirational quotes and little positive exercises to help you find a little 'perfect' in every day! My quest was that the journal would 'Make A Difference' and if it helped even just one person then it would have done its job. It is doing its job now and helping many. I still get visits from the black dog, but he is more controllable and less fierce. I hope that my journal will continue to help others in taming this horrible, vile beast.

Thank you!

Ali Gill - Hidden Perfects

www.hiddenperfects.co.uk

If you try getting into the habit of writing your own daily 'perfect', in a year's time you would have accumulated 365 things to be grateful for!

Examples of things that I currently feel grateful for...

1) ____________________

2) ____________________

3) ____________________

4) ____________________

5) ____________________

6) ____________________

7) ____________________

8) ____________________

9) ____________________

10) ____________________

## My thoughts about having 'gratitude for the small things' in my life…

*'My feet will want to walk to where you are sleeping but I shall go on living.'*

***~ Pablo Neruda***

# Emerging Back Into Life

There will be a time when you emerge back into some form of 'normality' and only you will know when the time feels right to do this. 'Normality' will vary from person to person and it may relate to when you return to your job or business following your bereavement or alternatively, it may be when you feel ready to go out and socialise with friends. You may feel quite anxious and emotional to start with, especially if you are faced with being frequently asked how you are feeling. Meeting people after the loss of a loved one can be awkward for all concerned. We have probably all been in a situation when you want to ask how someone is following their bereavement but don't want to overly upset them too.

If you have experienced grief in the past, try to recall how you got through those difficult times before and if appropriate, try to manage this bereavement in a similar way. If you found that you didn't cope well previously, you may want to analyse what you struggled with and where possible, do things differently this time.

It is often said that we are stronger than we give ourselves credit for, so spend time concentrating on your strengths and incorporate them into your life as frequently as possible to help you move on.

Here are some examples of personal strengths...

Courageous Thoughtful Trustworthy Caring Patient
Inspirational Enthusiastic Dedicated Adventurous
Practical Friendly Independent Gracious Determined
Organised Authentic Out-going Helpful

Listed below are examples on how you can use your 'strengths' to their full advantage when emerging back into life.

**Adventurous** - set yourself a new challenge, for example do a mountain hike like Snowdonia in Wales

**Caring** - visit or help a vulnerable person, for example do some gardening for an elderly neighbour

**Determined** - conquer a new pastime however challenging this may be, for example learn to speak a foreign language

**Inspirational** - turn a bad experience into a positive outcome, for example write a book about your experiences with dementia

**Practical** - make something useful, for example knit hats for your local premature baby unit

# My Personal Strengths are...

1)

2)

3)

4)

5)

How I can use these strengths to help me emerge back into life:

1) ____________________

____________________

____________________

____________________

2) ____________________

____________________

____________________

____________________

3) ____________________

____________________

____________________

____________________

4) ______________________________________________

______________________________________________

______________________________________________

______________________________________________

5) ______________________________________________

______________________________________________

______________________________________________

______________________________________________

We can also be victims of our own weaknesses, so it is important to recognise and accept what they are, as you may not always be able to overcome them. If your weaknesses start to have a detrimental effect on you, then you may need to seek professional help to minimise or lessen the impact they are having on your life.

Examples of Weaknesses...

Anxious Emotional Sensitive Self-critical Negative
Pessimistic Worrier Cynical Overwhelmed
Procrastination

# My own weaknesses are...

1)

2)

3)

4)

5)

I can prevent each of these weaknesses having a detrimental effect on my life by...

1) ______________________________________________

______________________________________________

______________________________________________

______________________________________________

2) ______________________________________________

______________________________________________

______________________________________________

______________________________________________

3) ______________________________________________

______________________________________________

______________________________________________

______________________________________________

4) ______________________________________________

______________________________________________

______________________________________________

______________________________________________

5) ______________________________________________

______________________________________________

______________________________________________

______________________________________________

## Any further thoughts I have on 'emerging back into life'…

______________________________________________

______________________________________________

______________________________________________

______________________________________________

______________________________________________

______________________________________________

# Living in the Present

I'm a big believer that you should always try to live your life in the present. Events from the past can't be changed, even though you may now feel remorseful about how you behaved or reacted to a previous experience. It is important to gain some form of closure and release any limiting beliefs that you may still be holding on to. Recognise that none of us are perfect. We are only 'human' and many of us have said and done things in our lives that we probably now regret. With this in mind, we are often left with two choices to either dwell on past events and risk digging an even deeper 'pit of remorse' or we can learn from previous mistakes and move on with our lives.

In a similar way to past events, we also have no control over our future. Situations and people can be unpredictable. What we think may happen or want to happen may not always occur. This can leave us despondent and disappointed that our life is not living up to our expectations. I personally support the theory that things often happen for a reason, which can be a 'bitter pill to swallow' when times are tough. It is often difficult to find a person who can genuinely say that they have led a trouble-free life. Difficult and demanding situations will often make us stronger, especially if we take on board the positive learnings when we move forward. Experiencing the roller coaster of challenges associated with your dementia journey and subsequent bereavement is no exception to this rule.

With this in mind I urge you to take each day as it comes. During 'tougher' times you may need to break the day down even further to every hour, minute and second if this is required to help keep you afloat. Reward yourself for every difficult moment conquered and always remember that tomorrow is a new day with a fresh start.

## My thoughts on 'living in the present'...

# PLANS FOR YOUR FUTURE

It's important to plan for your future, as this will give you something to look forward to. With this in mind, you may decide to treat yourself to a holiday, a weekend away or arrange some special evenings out.

Alternatively, you could have made a major decision in your life, like moving from your current home. Perhaps it now holds too many painful memories, it could be time to downsize to something more manageable or maybe you just want to make a fresh start.

You may want to take planning for your future one step further by setting some ambitious goals. For example, you could look into starting a new business, save up to fly across the other side of the world to visit family or go back to education and learn a new vocation.

Sharing your loved one's dementia journey may have taught you that life is too short. None of us know what our futures may hold, so with this in mind you may want to consider putting together a 'bucket list' of things you would like to do before you die. For example, swim with the dolphins, fly in a hot air balloon or see the Northern Lights.

# A bucket list of the top 10 things I would like to do before I die

1) ______________________________

2) ______________________________

3) ______________________________

4) ______________________________

5) ______________________________

6) ______________________________

7) ______________________________

8) ______________________________

9) ______________________________

10) ______________________________

Whatever your individual circumstances are and whatever you endeavour to do in the future, make sure that the decisions you make feel right for you. A good indication that you are on the right path is when you feel happy and excited for your planned events to arrive.

## Any further thoughts I may have about 'making plans for the future'…

# Finding Your Inner Strength

It always amazes me how people can find remarkable strength in the light of a tragic event which may have affected them badly. A tragedy like the Grenville Tower disaster comes to mind, where those involved showed superhuman strength by helping one another, when many of them had lost so much themselves.

There are also many 'inner strength' stories, found in articles and television documentaries associated with people who may have found courage to go on after the death of a child, a family murder or a tragic accident involving a loved one. Such family members going through a traumatic bereavement may have gone beyond courage to campaign for changes in the law, raised funds or heighten media awareness.

Although you may not always immediately recognise it, you too, will have an inner strength. You will find it, if you search hard enough; it just may not feel like you do at this moment in time. Alternatively, you may have already had to find strength to carry on, especially if your family rely on you to be 'their rock'. This may be in the case of an elderly parent or a young family.

# My thoughts on 'finding my inner strength'...

*'You've got to trust yourself. Be gentle with yourself. And listen to yourself. You're the only person who can get through this now.'*

**~ Tessa Shaffer**

# ONWARDS AND UPWARDS

We are now coming to the end of this book with what I hope is a greater understanding into your own personal grief process, as well as strategies that you can adopt in helping you move positively forward with your own life.

My overall aim with this book, 'Gone But Not Forgotten' has been to help and support you throughout each section, as you travel through your own unique bereavement journey. It is essential that you always recognise that you are never alone with the thoughts and feelings that you are experiencing. 'Events' in our life will always test us. In light of this, certain experiences will prove to be more challenging to live through than others. The bereavement of your loved one will be no exception. You may always have your good and bad days however, it is hoped in time, that the good days will outweigh the bad.

Endeavour to take small steps to move on with your life and accept that sometimes you will inevitably take steps back. You may often feel that facing a life without your loved one is too unbearable to envisage, as you will always inevitably miss them. Create a new future for yourself the best way possible, as your loved one would of course, be also wishing for you to do this.

Avoid spending too much time dwelling on what has gone on in the past, especially if their dementia illness has left you with some unpleasant memories. As I have said at the very beginning of this book, experiencing dementia with a loved one exposes you to a double bereavement, occurring both during and after their illness. However, it's now finally time for you to have some inner peace. Take the brave steps to move forward by pushing away any negative thoughts that enter your mind and instead replace them with only happy memories that bring a smile to your face. Never underestimate the courage, strength and determination you do have to get through this. Place trust in your journey, live in the moment and give yourself plenty of things to look forward to, as you travel onwards and upwards!

## My final thoughts about moving 'onwards and upwards'...

# Final Words

As the book title suggests, your loved one may be 'gone but not forgotten'. Continue to hold on to the love you have for them, as they will always have a special place in your heart. Keep their memory alive by remembering the good times with a smile. Life may never be the same following your experience with dementia, as this illness often leaves an imprint on the lives of those left behind. Bad experiences can often outweigh the happy memories you shared before the illness began, making your bereavement more challenging to deal with. The road ahead may at times feel 'rocky', however you will find an inner strength to move forward if you place trust in your own unique journey.

My best wishes, as always

Tracy x

# Further Thoughts

# Addendum – Coronavirus

Since originally writing this book and before it went for publishing, the world was faced with a pandemic. Not one of us could fully comprehend the impact it would have on our own lives and those of our loved ones. Due to the enormity of this situation, I did not want to end my book without mentioning it.

COVID-19 has had such a devasting effect on the care industry and especially in our hospitals and care homes. Many people who have loved ones with dementia have lost them prematurely due to this virus.

Some of you may have lost loved ones during this pandemic even though it may have not been COVID-19 related. Losing someone during this time may have meant that you were not allowed to see them in the final days and hours leading up to their death, due to lockdown restrictions.

If this pandemic did have an impact on you, either through the loss of your loved one or your subsequent bereavement, you may find it beneficial to write any thoughts and feelings below.

---

---

## AND FINALLY…

### Our Memories Build a Special Bridge

*Our memories build a special bridge*
*When loved ones have to part*
*To help us feel we're with them still*
*And soothe a grieving heart.*
*They span the years and warm our lives*
*Preserving ties that bind;*
*Our memories build a special bridge*
*And bring us peace of mind.*

***~ Emily Matthews***

# REFERENCES

Links to sites with poetry and hymns referred to in this book:

www.funeralhymnsheets.co.uk/popular-funeral-hymns

www.naturalendings.co.uk/funeral-poetry

www.funeralzone.co.uk/blog/10-inspirational-quotations-about-grief

www.funeralzone.co.uk/blog/top-funeral-hymns

www.goodreads.com/quotes/tag/bereavement

www.hearttoheartsympathygifts.com/sympathy-messages-quotes.html

https://bit.ly/ECondolences

*****

## Acknowledgements

Many thanks to everyone that contributed to this book:

Ali Gill www.hiddenperfects.co.uk

Dawn Hardy

Jane Moore https://bit.ly/DementiaNellieDean

Lynn Robinson www.lynn-robinson-medium.co.uk

Paula www.memorybearsfromtheheartbypaula.co.uk

*****

Tracy Gough

http://www.makewayfortomorrow.com

My Dementia Journey
Available on Amazon: http://bit.ly/MyDementiaJourney

Twitter.com/TracyEGough

Printed in Great Britain
by Amazon

58490599R00145